SELF PUBLISHING IN CANADA

A complete guide to designing, printing and selling your book

Other books by Suzanne Anderson:

*Good Morning Quadra: The History of the
HMCS Quadra*

SELF PUBLISHING IN CANADA

A complete guide to designing, printing and selling your book

Suzanne Anderson

Second Edition, Revised

Half Acre Publishing
Duncan, British Columbia

Canadian Cataloguing in Publication Data

Anderson, Suzanne 1953-
    Self-Publishing in Canada: a complete guide
    to designing, printing and selling your book/
    Suzanne Anderson.--2nd ed.

Includes bibliographical references and index.
ISBN 978-1-894208-03-1

    1. Self-publishing--Canada I. Title.

    Z285.5.A54 2011 070.5'930971
    C2011-903117-5

Cover design by Spica Design, Victoria, BC

Half Acre Publishing
3321 Renita Ridge Road
Duncan, British Columbia V9L5J6

Printed in Canada

Dedication

To all the writers who have chosen to self-publish their own books, and especially my friend and mentor T.W. Paterson who has done it more than twenty times.

TABLE OF CONTENTS

CHAPTER ONE
The Writer's Dream 1
    The dream • Why self publish • Types
    of publishers • Financing

CHAPTER TWO
All the Technical Stuff 21
    Choosing a subject • Title • Pen name •
    Editing • Book design • Front cover •
    Back cover • Front material • Main
    body of the book • Back matter • Order
    form

CHAPTER THREE
Make it Legal 75
    Getting ready • Copyright • ISBN • CIP
    • New Book Service • Bowkerlink •
    Legal Deposit • Barcodes • How to set
    the price • Putting it all together

CHAPTER FOUR
Building a Book 93
Typesetting • You or an expert? • Doing
it yourself • Typography • Font •
Printing process • Printers and
estimates • Types of printers • E-books
• Proof copy • Binding • After your
books are printed

CHAPTER FIVE
Your Self-Publishing Business 117
Home based business • Name • GST/
HST • Bank account • Bookkeeping •
Credit cards • PayPal

CHAPTER SIX
Before the Release Date 131
Pre-publication • Marketing plan •
Lists and databases • Reviews •
Information sheets • Media packages •
News releases • Advertising

CHAPTER SEVEN
Books for Sale! 151
Marketing • Word of mouth • Direct
mail • Ads • Website • Bookstores –
real and online • Book signings •
Libraries • Wholesalers • Distributors •
Book clubs • Foreign sales • Other
sales

CHAPTER EIGHT
Getting Them Out 175
Fulfilling orders • Invoices • Payment
terms • Consignment

CHAPTER NINE
More Possibilities 185
Afterward • Selling rights • Articles •
Public speaking • Workshops and
seminars • Booklets and reports •
Awards • Publishers • Remainders

CHAPTER TEN
Success Stories 199
Jean Paré • David Chilton • Greta and
Janet Podleski • Dania Lebovics •
Virginia Brucker • Joe Garner

APPENDICES
Checklist 207
Associations for writers 210
Websites for writers 213

GLOSSARY 216

BIBLIOGRAPHY 235

INDEX 238

FOREWORD

I don't want people to die with a book still inside them.
—Dan Poynter

When I started self-publishing 34 years ago, I had to learn the hard way - by trial and error. Since then I have made it my personal quest to make sure that anyone who wants to publish their own book learns how to do it right. I have written several books on the subject and lecture worldwide.

I believe in self-publishing as the best way to get your book out to the public. You will make more money, which everyone wants, get to press sooner and have complete control of your book. This is more important than you realize. You should be the one who picks out the book's title and decides where to sell your book. After all, bookstores are not necessarily the best places to sell books. Who will know your market better than you?

While Canada and the United States have much in common, there are enough differences in resources and business practices to merit this book. I believe Canada needs a book like this. Right now more and more people are starting to self-publish. With the information gathered from this, and other books, you will acquire the knowledge to do it professionally and successfully.

Dan Poynter
The Self Publishing Manual
Author-publisher who has coached thousands of successful publishers

PREFACE

When I wrote the first edition of *Self Publishing in Canada*, I had no idea how much the face of publishing would change in seven years. E-readers, smart phones, blogs, Facebook and Twitter were either not around or not used by the common people. Now they are an integral part of our society, in particular for anyone who is marketing a product such as a book. I decided that *Self Publishing in Canada* had to be updated to reflect new information.

It is estimated that more than 10,000 books are self-published in Canada every year and now even more Canadians need this comprehensive guide to the process. People need to know about GST/HST, business startup, marketing strategies, and especially Canadian resource lists. Most importantly people need to understand how differently copyright, ISBN, and CIP data are handled in Canada.

Self-publishing has become more than a choice in the publishing world, it is becoming the preference of many entrepreneurs. More people want control of their books and believe they understand the best way to market them. More authors want to reap the rewards of their work. Unfortunately, the biggest hurdle for most writers is that they do not know how to publish their own books. They do not know how to make a product that can compete with the trade published books on the shelves. As more writers turn to self-publishing, this book will help fill that gap.

CHAPTER ONE

The Writer's Dream

Listen and learn and find your dream.
When you have found it, don't give up.
— Alwyn Morris

THE DREAM

Most writers dream of the day when they will see their book in print. The scene unfolds with a letter from a publisher offering to purchase your manuscript. You work with a professional editor who helps you turn the manuscript into the best writing you could ever imagine doing. An array of professionals design the pages and covers, and a whole department is available to market your book. All you have to do is revise and rewrite if necessary. When all these people get finished with your manuscript - it is a book! It becomes your success story and sells in bookstores. This dream keeps many new writers going.

The reality is that you send queries to publisher after publisher after publisher. You receive letters thanking you, BUT your book is not right for their list for one reason or another. That is assuming you even receive a reply. You might have a book for an audience you are familiar with and write great letters pitching ideas for promotion, but there simply are not enough publishers to print all the manuscripts in Canada. It is estimated that only 1 in 10 manuscripts will get into print. The dream begins to sound like a nightmare. But do not despair. There is a way to become published.

WHY SELF-PUBLISH

If you are reading this book, the events I describe are probably familiar to you. You, like many others, have decided that if no one is willing to publish your book then you will do it yourself. You believe strongly in what you have written and want to make it available to others – to readers. You will take the chance and, if it arrives, the money and fame.

Many well-known authors and books come from the self-publishing field. Mark Twain, A.A. Milne, Lord Byron, Edgar Allen Poe, and Beatrix Potter were all self-published. More recently *The Celestine Prophecy, The Christmas Box,* and *Bridges of Madison County* started out as self-published books which were picked up by a trade publisher and went on to become international bestsellers. *The Wealthy Barber, Company's Coming* cookbooks and *The Looney Spoons Cookbook* series are Canadian self-published books that have become best sellers. Unfortunately there is a stigma to self-publishing. It has been felt for too long that people publish their own books because they are not good enough for a "real" publisher to handle it. Self-publishing has long been thought of as the place of last resort for rejected writers. Well they are wrong! In the next decade, more and more of our reading material will come from author-publishers. As computer technology improves, and the trade publishers become even more dollar driven, a whole new niche is opening up for people who are willing to do it themselves. Self-publishing is quickly becoming a chosen option.

Self-publishing is both demanding and gratifying. You have control of the whole program. You design the cover, choose the price, and decide where and when the book will be distributed. You start your own publishing company and may be able to take advantage of tax deductions. Of course you have already been doing this as a writer, haven't you? (Talk to an accountant about it). The really neat thing about self-publishing is that you get to keep all the money you make on the book.

The standard royalty contract with an

established publishing company gives a first time writer 7 - 10% on the book (retail) price. Sometimes you can get a bit higher percentage if it is paid on the wholesale price. Unless you are already famous, the advance will barely cover the expenses you incurred researching and writing your book. Then you will only receive a royalty cheque once or twice a year, and not necessarily in the first year. With self-publishing you start making money with the first book you sell. Except for production expenses, the money is all yours.

One of the major advantages to self-publishing is the amount of time it takes to turn your manuscript into a book. It is possible to have your books ready to sell in less than eight weeks. A traditional publisher could take as long as one or two years to make this happen. The sooner your books are available for sale, the sooner you start making money.

When you self-publish, you retain all the rights to your book. Many potential authors do not realize that the trade publisher will own the right to print their book. Since they put out the funds to have it published, this is part of their pay off. It is fair, but many find it frustrating that a book they spent months, or even years, working on will not even legally belong to them. All they have is the copyright. This leads us to the fact that self-publishers have full control over their work. A person who self-publishes makes all the decisions concerning editing, content, cover, title, and marketing. Often new authors working with a trade publisher for the first time are shocked to find out they have no control over what their book will be titled, what it will look like or how it will be organized. Self-publishing sounds all too easy. And maybe it is. It is also time consuming, costs money, and has its own language. Self-publishing appears deceptively simple – format your manuscript, design a cover and have a printer put the whole thing together. In fact, it is a complex operation that can be intimidating to a novice. What this book hopes to do is explain the whole process to you. I recommend that you first read this book from cover to cover. Only then will you know what you are up against. After you know the facts, you can then make an informed decision as to whether you want to go through with self-publishing your book. Never forget this is a business. By doing your homework, you should not end up as one of the many businesses in this country that fail every year.

TYPES OF PUBLISHERS

Trade Publishers

There are many kinds of publishers. The most well known are the big ones such as McClelland & Stewart Inc, whose stable of authors ranges from Margaret Atwood to

Alice Munro. They are the big players in the Canadian publishing industry. They produce the most best-sellers and have the largest publicity budgets. Because of the cost of competition and producing books, they are not able to give new authors as much of a chance as they could many years ago.

There are medium and small publishers who take more chances with the kinds of books that the large publishers cannot afford to do. These usually are literary books or specialty books that appeal to a smaller, or niche, audience. Small presses allow the writer more input into the production, marketing, and distribution of their book, however, these days even the small publishers are driven by the cost of producing and marketing a book.

In the trade publishing industry, too many books are being produced because the marketing department decides what will sell. A novice author can be disillusioned to discover this. For most of this century, editors have discovered new authors, designers have made a product appealing to the reading public, and the marketing department has sold the books. In the past few years it seems that editors and designers have to make decisions based on what the marketing department thinks will sell well and not only recover the cost of production, but make a profit. This is getting harder and harder to do.

Bookstores are changing too. In the

past few years, the small local bookstores that welcomed regional books are being pushed aside by the large chain stores. Known as "box" stores, they have enormous floor space and usually support a coffee bar or café and sell other retail items besides books. These types of bookstores are expensive to run because they try to open in prime retail sites. They cannot afford to carry stock that is not selling for very long. Unsold books are returned to the publisher (who already sold it for a discount) for a full refund. Trade publishing is a tough industry.

University Presses

Many Canadian universities operate small publishing houses. They release from six to thirty titles a year. The one exception is University of Toronto Press with 125 to 130 releases a year. They tend to publish nonfiction, primarily scholarly or trade books, and literary fiction. Check under Book Publishers in *The Canadian Writer's Market* for details on what each press is looking for. Perhaps your manuscript will fall into a subject area covered by a university press, and you can have your book published for you. Keep in mind that the university presses are still in the same situation as trade publishers. In other words, they need to make a profit.

Subsidy Publishing

If you want to be published badly enough, and have lots of money, you can pay someone to do it for you. The country is full of subsidy or print-on-demand (POD) publishers who will produce a book for you. These types of publishers are often referred to in the industry as "vanity publishers" because some people will pay anything to see their name in print. I personally do not like this term because it is not really relevant in this century. Anyone with a computer can produce their own book or booklet and the concept of vanity does not come into it anymore. We are in an information age and producing books and booklets is a way to impart information.

For a pre-paid sum of money the subsidy publisher assists you with ordering required information for your legal page, prints your book, sends one or two books to the National Book Deposit, puts your book into their online bookstore, and give you a "complimentary" five or ten books. You need to be aware that the legal page information is free in Canada and that postage to send two books to the National Book Deposit will cost less than $20.00. You will have to pay printing costs no matter what route you take and you have to pay extra fees for editing, typesetting and cover design. Also ask yourself when was the last time you purchased a book from a subsidy publisher's

THE WRITERS DREAM   9

online bookstore. While it sounds great to begin with, it is by no means a good marketing tool.

If you want more books, you have to pay for them. While the concept of "one book as you need it" is what POD promotes, they still charge a lot less per unit when you buy several books. This is what you would expect from a regular offset printer, which the subsidy companies claim are more expensive. They also insist you use their publishing name and issue you with an ISBN from their list, which means you lose control of your book. Recently, some subsidies are trying to copyright the book design so you cannot go elsewhere.

Unfortunately, there are many subsidies that charge the author too much money and develop an inferior product. Many book reviewers will not even read a book with a subsidy press label on it. Subsidy publishers require a lot of research. Although the first place to find one is under *Publishers* in the Yellow Pages, the next place to go is the Better Business Bureau, and then online. Subsidy publishers do not give your manuscript the benefit of good editing, although you can have that service for an extra fee for a contract editor. They do not guarantee a good product either. Often the books fall apart easily. If you choose to deal with this type of publisher, remember that you are paying for a product they have no interest in selling. After spending a large sum of money, you still have to market your book yourself.

All that being said, a subsidy publisher might be right for you. It will depend on what you plan to do with your book. If you are putting together a family history or a chapbook of poetry that you do not plan to sell widely to the general public, then this might be your best option. If you only plan on a short run of books to be given away or sold in a small local market, this might be a solution for you. You decide what you want and then you receive a product to give to family or friends. Whether a reviewer will look at it or not is of no importance. Subsidy publishing does fill a need.

Desktop Publishing

Often people in a desktop publishing center have years of publishing experience and walk the new author through the process with expert advice along the way. They have in-house resources such as designers and typesetters, and act as a consultant during the process. Most do not print books, but will help you find a printer. They do not help you market your book either. Fees vary, so make sure you check out at least three DTP centers and compare prices to services. Be sure to have the company show you other books they have helped to publish so you can check for quality. Like printing companies, not all DTP centers have experience with books.

Book Production Companies

Unlike the Desktop Publishing companies, these folks work with the new author until the book is actually in print. Some even help market your book. They charge a flat fee per book. Although there are reputable companies of this kind, be careful when you deal with them. Some companies charge the flat rate and then add on extra fees. One new author had her bill increase by 50% by the time she received her books. Make sure you understand the contract. When in doubt, see a lawyer. One visit will not cost you thousands of dollars, but that is what it could save you.

As with subsidy publishers, check to see what imprint or publisher's name will be on the book. If you intend to truly self publish, you will want to have your own publishing name in the book. Do not share the publishing rights either. You want full control and ownership of your book.

Co-op Publishing

Sometimes several people get together to pool their skills and produce a book or several books. They share the work right up to the printing process. This can save money on editing, design, typesetting, and layout. Then the group shares the cost of marketing. This group form of self-publishing requires less individual financial investment. Before getting involved with co-op publishing, make sure everyone's part is spelled out clearly. More importantly, be clear on the financial obligation of every member of the group. Spell out any profit sharing. Misunderstandings can cause hard feelings among members of the group, which will defeat the original purpose and affect productivity. A smart move would to see a lawyer before setting it up.

E-Publishing

Online publishing firms purchase manuscripts, pay royalties, and make writers' books available to the public just like a traditional trade publisher. In this case, though, they do not print your book on paper, but make it available on the internet. Customers are often able to read the beginning of the book for free and decide if they want to download it. They can purchase it and download it immediately. This makes that "first impression" – the first chapter – necessary to be your very best writing in order to hook a purchaser (of course, it should be anyway). The e-book is purchased online, and that is how authors are able to receive royalties. Since the cost of production and paper is not necessary, there is usually a profit to pay the royalties out of.

Like any publisher, you have to do your homework and check out the online publishing companies. Some offer a straight deal like you would receive from a regular trade publisher, and others offer to share the financial cost. Check to see what types of computers and readers the firm can download it to. It is important for an e-publishing firm to keep up with the latest technology in order to make your book available to the greatest number of readers. A good e-publisher should have editors who will work with you the same as that of a trade publisher. Most e-publishers are one-person or small operations. Make sure they have the skills to do the job.

Some writers prefer to produce their own e-books. Remember, the book still has to be formatted properly and you need to decide what e-book reader market you want to reach. At the very least, the book should be available in PDF format. Every day more e-book readers are coming on the market and the price is rapidly decreasing. Consider an electronic version of your book to complement the print version. It gets its own ISBN and allows you to offer your book to a whole other type of reader.

Self-publishing

A concept that has been around for centuries, self-publishing has been made even easier with the development of computer technology. You can produce a manuscript with word processing software that will give you, among other things, word count, sentence length, font type, and even set up your titles and subtitles. In the newer word processing programs you can completely format your text. This means you can set up such things as page size, font type and size, page numbers, the table of contents, and chapter heads. Some even have the ability to make an index. If you know how to use a desktop publishing program such as *Quark*, *PageMaker* or *InDesign*, you can format even more professionally. Both of these methods will take you to the point where you produce a *galley*. These days a galley is no longer hard copy. Printers will require your formatted manuscript saved as a Portable Document Format (PDF) file. You can do this by downloading one of the many free online PDF maker programs. Computers make self-publishing an attainable goal for everyone. If you do not know how to use one, you probably have a friend or family member who does. And for those who view the new technology with real trepidation, you can still hire someone to typeset and format your manuscript. Just make sure they save it as a PDF file.

As an author-publisher you are in control of the whole process from beginning to end. This gives you much greater opportunity to be creative. After all, you wrote the book so you should know best what to call it, what it should look like, and who would want to buy it. Unlike trade published books, you call

THE WRITERS DREAM   15

the shots on everything. For example, you might think you have the perfect title for your book. Trade publishers normally change the title of a book unless you are really insistent, which is not a good idea for a new author. By self-publishing, you do not have to make compromises.

When you self-publish, you decide how to market your book. Should it be marketed by mail order, online or through a distributor? If you want the latter, how do you find one? What is the purchase price of the book going to be? You might be able to hook up with a corporation that will want your book as a product tie-in to either sell or give away. You may be a natural salesperson. If so, you have a chance of being successful selling your books. If you, or someone you know, has computer skills you should build your own website. Most e-mail providers will give you web space. Sometimes it even comes for free with your account. Or purchase your own website. When I decided to write this book, I purchased **www. selfpublishing.ca** and held on to it until I was ready to develop it as part of my marketing plan. Today the site is a large part of my business. You may even have bought this book from the website.

You can have your books on the shelf much more quickly if you self-publish. It could take a trade publisher anywhere from one to three years to release a book. Publishing yourself could have it in your hands (or basement or garage) in as little as six to eight weeks. This puts it in the bookstore much more quickly and allows you to start making money more quickly, too.

One of the nicest things about self-publishing is that you will get to keep all the profits you make from the book. Since you are going to be in business for yourself, you can take advantage of income tax breaks. Of course many of these tax breaks were available to you as an author, but as a registered small business you can take advantage of even more tax opportunities. The best way to start out is by visiting an accountant for a consultation.

All this control and money sounds wonderful. Just remember, this is a small business with all the headaches that can come with it. While there are many positive aspects about being self-employed, you are still the one who is responsible for all decisions. If you the novice publisher make a mistake, then you the business person will pay for it. You will not have the services of a professional editor unless you hire one. You will not have the benefit of an experienced publicist unless you hire one. You may not have an artistic bone in your body so designing a cover could be a formidable task. There are not many books available on how to design book covers, so you would have to either take your chances or hire a graphic designer. Designing the interior of the book may be a large job too. Again, you can hire someone to format the book for you or muddle through yourself. Remembering that an amateur looking book will not sell very well, you then have to decide if you want to spend money on professionals or risk losing money on an unpopular product. Either way, it is going to cost you money.

FINANCING

When you self-publish you have to have the funds to pay up front for the book's production. This amount can vary from hundreds to several thousands of dollars. First you have to find the funding to produce the book. Then you have to spend money and work hard to market the book. Otherwise you will end up with boxes and boxes - and boxes - of books stored in your house or garage. This leads you to doubt your book and your ability to write. But it may not be your writing you should question, just your uninformed decisions.

So where does one find money to become a self-publisher? There are many sources. Some of them might work for you and others definitely will not. The most obvious place to start is with yourself. If you have money in savings, a line of credit, or can take out a second mortgage on your home you can come up with the funds. You might see if you can get a loan from the bank or your credit card, but this will saddle you with payments before you have a chance to sell any books. Another source would be family members who are either willing to loan the money or would become a partner in this venture. It is doubtful if you would find investors unless you plan on going into publishing in a big way. If you receive money from someone other than yourself or your family, go to a lawyer and have a contract drawn up. This could save a lot of grief in the future.

The most well known story of financing a self-published book is about Ottawa sisters Janet and Greta Podleski who co-wrote the best-selling cookbook *Looneyspoons*. They both quit their jobs to work on the project. They used up their savings, maxed out their credit cards, and sold just about everything they owned of value - including Janet's car. They even had an enormous bake sale to raise money. In their case, the risk paid off handsomely. Not only was their book a bestseller in both Canada and the United States, they have published two more cookbooks. They write a monthly section in *Reader's Digest* magazine and host a television show on Food Network Canada.

There is no easy way to put it - you have to spend money to self-publish. The actual amount will depend on the trim size and page count of your book. The number of books you decide to print will make up your largest cost.

Like in any small business, one misstep can be expensive. Before you start self-publishing, you have to learn as much as you can about this particular business. If you have no experience in business at all, you have to learn about that too. If you are not a patient person, and do not want to study either publishing or business, you could lose money.

Self-publishing can be the most gratifying thing you do in your life. The thrill of seeing your book in print and on bookshelves is tremendous. At the same time it could become the biggest and most expensive nightmare of your life. Take your time to learn the business and you will have a good chance at success. You may not make a lot of money, but you will be able to proudly tell others you are an author. This is great for a writer's confidence. When starting out, most of us feel uncomfortable telling people we are writers. They immediately want to know what we have written. Once you publish your book, you will now realize that you are a "real" writer and not just a "wannabe". You can proudly take your place alongside other Canadian authors, whether famous or not. Each one of us contributes to Canada's heritage. And hey, isn't that worth taking a chance on?

CHAPTER TWO

All That Technical Stuff

For us, fantasy is just reality waiting
for a technology to give it birth.

— Frank Zingrone

PICK A SUBJECT

Some topics work better for self-publishing than others. Non-fiction, how-to and poetry books work especially well. This is not to mean you cannot produce good fiction or a children's illustrated book. But they are tough to market. Right now memoirs, regional histories, and self-help are hot topics to write about. They lend themselves well to being self-published because they can be done in small print runs if necessary. These books tend to be of interest to a smaller market, which makes them ideal for self-publishing. Many trade publishers, whether large or small, cannot afford to take on a project with a small market. It is just not financially feasible for them.

When you pick your subject, remember you will have to know as much or more about it than anyone who might read your book. In other words, you have to become an expert. Readers expect you to have done all the research. They expect you to be very knowledgeable about the subject. I cannot stress how important it is that you do not let them down. The first book I wrote was the history of a Naval training facility known as a "stone ship." I spent three full years researching and writing the book. Unless you are writing a memoir (from memory) you have to learn as much detail about your subject as possible in order to give your reader the full benefit of the material. Skimp on this and people will not want to read your book. Worse, present less than well-researched material and you will receive unflattering reviews, which means people will still not want to read your book. Any way you look at it, poor preparation will lead to low book sales.

Not many of us have the luxury of hiring a professional researcher. Chances are you are reading this book because you have already written something and have had no success with a trade publisher picking up your manuscript. Take the time to go over your manuscript carefully. Check your sources fully - and then recheck them. It is very embarrassing to have a glaring mistake mentioned in either a review or a letter from a reader. If you want to publish more than one book, you want to build up a cadre of fans of your writing such as Joe Garner did with his books. You do not want all of your fan mail to be full of corrections, you want it to be full of glowing testimonials.

Non-fiction

In the world of small publishing, it is often said you should find a niche and fill it. That is what I have done with this book. When I was researching about how to self-publish my first book, I discovered there is only one nationally well-known book on the subject specific to Canada. I felt there was room for more. In the United States, there are well over fifty books on self-publishing that I could find and presumably there are many more that I did not find. If you figure that Canada has about one-tenth of the population of the U.S., it stands to reason there should be room for more books. Every writer has a different voice, different knowledge, and a different slant on how to present the material. That is one of the joys of writing. Some excellent American self-publishing guides are full of material that is not country specific. In fact, you should read several books on self-publishing before you start on your own venture. If you subscribe to the theory that you can never know too much, you will only benefit from studying a multitude of resources. The books I used to research this book are listed in the Bibliography in the back matter. Remember, though, these are only the books I read. I also read trade magazines and took publishing courses.

Non-fiction is a very broad area, which is why trade publishers cannot publish every manuscript they receive. Writers often have a specific skill or have done some tremendous research on subjects of interest. If the book fills a niche, it may be a small one. It may not lend itself to a short-term marketable project that will carry itself financially. Publishers also hesitate to pick up work of unknown authors. Remember, trade publishers cannot afford to carry either a book or an author that is not paying its way. That is the reality of the business these days.

You might have knowledge or interest in a specialized topic. Your target audience may be small or select, and you may think it is fine if you do not make the best seller list. If you are content to have steady sales over the long term, you might be an ideal candidate to self-publish.

Creative non-fiction

A new way of presenting non-fiction to a reader is by writing creative non-fiction. The author uses literary style and fiction technique to write the creative non-fiction. Attention is paid to writing style, scene, and narrative.

Recognized as a genre, it includes personal essays, memoir, travel writing, food writing, biography and literary journalism. When a non-fiction book follows an actual story arc, is it often referred to as narrative non-fiction. Right now there are few established conventions because is it such a new genre. Make sure you understand what you are doing before writing non-fiction this way. It might be a good idea to start with short stories or articles.

How-to books

The how-to book is in the non-fiction category, but is more specialized. If you have a skill and want to share your knowledge with others, this is the category for you. *The Wealthy Barber* by David Chilton is a how-to book. So are many popular cookbooks. Interestingly, there is still a large market for cookbooks. To be properly illustrated they can be costly to produce, but the success of the *Company's Coming* cookbook series is unsurpassed in Canadian publishing.

Let us say you are a great cook or woodworker or gardener or craftsperson. You can write and publish a book about the subject you specialize in. You would be considered a specialist in that skill and others might be interested in reading what you have to say or what you have to teach. Take a minute now and think about the skills you have. Is there something that you seem to always be showing your friends or family how to do? Many traditional homemaking skills are popular. There never seems to be enough books about quilting, cross-stitch or knitting. If you have ever been asked to teach a class on something of this nature at your local school, it may be time for a book. Just be careful about the timeliness of the material. Crafts, especially, are a field where you have to make sure you are not behind the times, or your book will not sell. Currently scrapbooking is popular and it seems to be enduring over the long term.

One self-published friend of mine is an expert at tapping the west coast maples on Vancouver Island and making maple syrup. He gives lectures, writes articles, organizes events and sells both his books and his maple syrup. He has turned an idea into somewhat of an industry. Look at the broad view of your book and see if you can branch off into other ways to benefit financially from your writing.

Booklets are gaining in popularity. You can often find how-to booklets advertised in the classified sections of magazines. This is a good place to test the response to what you have to offer. We will go into that in greater detail in a later chapter.

Family histories

The hobby of genealogy is growing

daily. After spending much time and energy researching their family tree, many people want to put it into book form for the whole family to enjoy and keep. Self-publishing allows you to control the process so you will know exactly what the cost will be. You can pre-charge family members for the book so no one person is out of pocket while waiting for family members to pay for their copy.

Using the services of a subsidy publisher can work well with a family history. You do not have to start a publishing business or concern yourself with either learning a whole lot or marketing the book. You will be charged a flat fee for a certain number of books and there should be no surprises. Once you have a price, you can divide it up evenly among family members who want a copy. It is an easy way to provide a book for the members of the family to purchase.

If you have a special gift for storytelling, you might want to present your family history in that manner. This could create a small local market in the community or communities your family has lived in. This would be especially true if your family was, if not prominent, but even moderately well known in a particular region. For example, your great-great-grandfather might not have been the Mayor, but he might have run a corner store for 25 years. This makes him part of that community's history as well as your own family's history. Handled properly, the history becomes the story of a man and his life, or the story of several generations of a family. Allow your muse to be creative and you never know what you will come up with.

Regional Histories

Canada is jam-packed with fascinating history. Right now Canadians are keen to learn about it too. This has produced a fairly sizeable market for regional histories. These books could include the history of a neighborhood, a town, a ghost town, or even a logging or mining camp. You might have grown up in a small town or ethnic neighborhood whose story begs to be told. Your greatest sales will come within this community. You are more likely to have the local bookstore carry six copies than a large chain ordering 600. But regional histories have longevity. They are still selling a decade after you publish them. You cannot expect to make a large profit, but should be able to see steady long term sales. British Columbia author T.W. Paterson has written and self-published eighteen books about Vancouver Island history. The local bookstore sells hundreds of them each time a new one is released. He also writes a column in the local newspaper about the history of the area. People look for his latest book.

There are grants available for writing books about certain regions. Check *The*

Canadian Writer's Market for all grants available in Canada. Many provinces provide grants to encourage regional history to be written. Of course competition will be tough and you may be unknown, but it is worth a letter and a stamp. Take note that some grants prohibit self-published books from being eligible. I hope that as our independently published books become better put together, that stigma will lift. Right now many agencies and booksellers believe that self-published books are badly done. Unfortunately, they are too often right. Learn more about acceptable book design in chapters three and four.

Memoirs

Everyone has a story to tell. It does not matter if you are old or relatively young, you have a story. Many of our seniors who emigrated or fought in one of the wars have written about their experiences. People who have triumphed over a disease or a family tragedy are also writing about it. You, too, might have a story to tell.

Webster's Universal Dictionary defines *memoir* as: (n) an historical account based on personal experience; (pl) an autobiographical record. Often people read a memoir to feel like they are not alone as they too go through experiences that only you can write about. That is one of the joys of a memoir. No two people will experience an event exactly the same way. That leaves a lot of room for this type of book.

Aside from the historical aspect of a memoir, there is the sharing of an experience. Perhaps you lost a parent as a child, had an alcoholic spouse or have successfully lived with a learning disability. When you write about your experiences and the emotions you went through at the time, others can empathize with you. Books like this often help others with the same problem. Many times people feel alone under adverse circumstances, and books like this help show them that they really are not alone. One writer friend of mine wrote a memoir about her experience with her husband's Alzheimer's disease and it is being used in a university as a text. We all have problems and reading about how other's coped can be very uplifting.

The subjects I have mentioned here are not the only ones that are popular for self-publishing. Humour, self-awareness, spirituality, cookbooks, fitness, and diet books are very trendy these days. There is no barrier to what you can write about. Any subject is acceptable and you can be successful if you follow the proper steps to producing a book.

Fiction

Yes, you can self-publish fiction stories. It is not as easy to market or sell, but it has been successfully done. Normally in self-publishing, you target your audience and lay out an appropriate marketing plan. That is great for non-fiction. To market fiction, you have to take a different approach. Public readings are a big part of letting potential readers know about your book. If you write genre fiction, you will want to seek out associations, websites and even specialized online bookstores for your book.

Showcase your fiction book by either putting the first chapter on your website or include some excerpts of the book in your blog. This will show others your writing style and hopefully start a fan base. Fiction writers want to build up a cadre of fans to read their book and any others they write. Take a page from the pros and get the word out there. One of the great things about fiction is that it does not go out of style; it is not about the timeliness of a subject and can have longevity. Your book might take a little time to catch on with readers, but that is okay with fiction.

Poetry

Poetry is hard to sell even for the large publishers. Poetry is literary and it seems to be most popular primarily in literary and academic circles. The type of book commonly used for poetry is a called a *chapbook*. It is a Half Standard Letter (5 3/8" x 8 3/8") that is very thin and has a specific layout. The market for poetry is not very large, but every time you do a reading you have an opportunity to expand your audience and these are the people who will buy your book. This is another kind of book that could be taken to a subsidy publisher. They do small print runs and that can keep your costs down.

TITLE

One of both the best and the worst things about self-publishing is that you get to make up the book's title. Usually, when a book goes to a trade publisher, the editorial department makes it up. I know writers who have not been happy about the chosen title, but they normally do not get a vote. Suffice it to say that if you want your book published, you often have to bite your tongue. This is not the case in self-publishing. It is part of the control you have over your material.

On the other hand, it can be a blessing to have a professional decide on your title. It is an art, and not one that comes naturally to all people. Take a look at the title of this book. I wanted it to be clear and leave no doubt what the book was about. Most books on self-publishing have those words in the title. In my case, I wanted booksellers and readers to know this book is specific to Canada. But this is a straightforward reference book. Other types of books such as history, poetry, memoir and fiction need to be titled in a different way

so that it not only indicates what the book is about, but also attracts readers.
Sometimes titling a book is easy. Often it is not. And, unfortunately, a bad title can hurt a book's chances of being sold. The title should be fairly short. Try to keep it to five words or less. If your book is non-fiction, use a sub-title to give a clearer description of your book. Do not start your title with "Introduction to..." because thousands of books have that title and yours will not stand out. If your book is fiction or poetry, the title should tie into the theme. While this is not imperative, remember that you are just starting out and want to entice as many readers as possible. If you become a well-known author, you can use more literary license with your titles. Look at the publication *Books in Print* to see if the title you have chosen has been used for another book. While book titles are not copyrighted, you do not want the same title as another book or future purchasers might become confused.

The title is part of what a potential purchaser will look at in the seven seconds they spend on the front cover of your book. The working title you choose may seem very comfortable to you, but jarring to others. Brainstorm some title (and if necessary sub-title) ideas, and show them to people. Do not limit yourself to just friends and family either. Ask all kinds of people that you are acquainted with or do business with. If you really cannot come up with a title you are satisfied with, hire a professional to do it. This is too important to be left to chance.

PEN NAME

A pen name, or *nom de plume*, is the pseudonym an author uses to conceal their true identity. Often famous authors will use a pen name when writing in another genre than that which they are known for. Sometimes famous people will use a pen name because they do not want the book to be associated with what they do, or they do not want to use their fame to sell the book. Should you use a pseudonym? Probably not.

When you are an unknown author, you will only mask your identity. How do you expect to sell books if you do not give your real name? You actually want to garner fame, and that will not be possible if no one knows who you really are. If the book is something you want people to know about, members of the local community might recognize you and the word will get around. On the other hand, if your book is controversial in any way, having the locals recognize you could be embarrassing for you. In my experience, new author-publishers tend to use odd pen names anyway. Your old high school nickname is not likely appropriate either. My advice is that unless you are already well known in another field, do not consider using a pen name.

EDITING

After you have written a manuscript, it needs to be edited. There are basically two kinds of editing - substantive editing and copy-editing. Substantive editing is the process of finding ways to make that what you have written even better. It looks at the manuscript as a whole. Copy-editing is the line-by-line and word-by-word search for errors in the text. Done correctly and methodically, both types of editing will give your manuscript a professional look rather than one that advertises you as an amateur publisher. Professional editing will polish your book so it will hold its own with other books in the field that have been published by established trade publishers.

One of the drawbacks to self-publishing is that you do not have a professional trade publishing editor to help smooth out the rough spots or catch mistakes. If you can afford to hire one, this is the best route to go. Freelance editors advertise in publications like *Writer's Digest, Quill & Quire* or the Editorial Services section of *The Book Trade in Canada*. The Writer's Union of Canada (TWUC) **www. writersunion.ca** and the Editor's Association of Canada **www.editors.ca** offer editorial services and you can find a list of editors on their websites. Editing will not come cheaply, but a good editor can really help showcase your best writing.

With the fierce competition to find a publisher, many writers are now paying to have their manuscript professionally edited before submitting it to an agent or publisher. Agents are recommending professional editing to new writers in order to make their manuscript more saleable. You owe it to yourself and your readers to ensure your book is properly edited. If it is not, you will come to regret it.

Many writers believer they cannot afford a professional editor and that they need to look elsewhere. One place to start is the English department of your local high school, college or university. The teachers all have the education and training to assist you - some may even have the time. Colleges and universities might have advanced English students who are willing to do the work for a reasonable fee in order to put the project on their resume. The cost is something you have to work out with a prospective editor. If you have received estimates from freelance editors, you will have some idea what the top end price is. Then figure out what you can afford. Some editors charge by the page and others charge by the hour. With the latter you have to be clear how long it will take for the editing job to be done. Make sure you make up a simple contract to ensure costs do not run over. And remember, this fee is an expense so get a receipt and take it to your accountant at tax time. Actually, you do not have to be a publisher to use the deduction.

Full time writers can take advantage of editing deductions too.

If you are lucky and have a friend or family member who is well read, they might be willing to edit the manuscript for you. If you absolutely cannot find a teacher or professional, then this is the next best option to use. When you do it this way, though, you must be clear as to what you want edited. Otherwise, ideas may clash and hard feelings flare up. If you feel you are being criticized, take the manuscript back. No book is worth losing friends over. I have one friend who only reads my manuscripts for typographical errors and "the feel". I have her make a note in the margin if she encounters a section that is mentally jarring. You know what I am talking about - the part in a book that you reread because the text did not seem to make sense. This way she is not expected to edit the content of my material, but helps me find the rough spots.

Unless you have a great relationship, do not ask your spouse, partner or significant other to edit your manuscript. Like friends, this can lead to hard feelings. You do not want to endanger your relationship over a book. It is not worth it.

The other person who cannot edit your book is yourself. You are too close to the material. Having written and (I hope) rewritten the material, you cannot see it objectively. Every person who has self-edited has horror stories of things missed because they were the one who had written the original material. But, if there is no other choice, put the manuscript away for at least one month to distance yourself from it. Write other things such as poetry, short stories or articles to clear your mind of the manuscript's topic. Then take it out and attempt to edit it.

You cannot rely on your computer's spellchecker or grammar checker either. Many people have, to their embarrassment, found simple mistakes when they counted on their technology. Spell checkers often give American spellings. If this is okay with you, do not bother to change the set up feature to Canadian English. Unfortunately spellcheckers do not catch properly spelled words used incorrectly. For example, if you hold a key down too long and write *too* instead of *to*, the spellchecker will not pick it up, but it will be an error in your text.

You cannot rely on the grammar checker to catch these mistakes either. The average grammar checker has formats for student compositions, business writing, and technical or scientific writing. None of these will work for you. It is time consuming to go through a whole chapter or manuscript. You may get frustrated that the grammar checker does not understand your writing style. It is a good place to start, but should never be considered the final editing.

Good old-fashioned reading is the only way to edit. Print off a copy of your manuscript because you cannot do this on the computer. Copy-editing can be done by using a ruler and reading the text from the bottom of the page up to the top. Then you are not reading the material, but looking at it line by line and word by word. Copy-editing needs to be done meticulously. It is time consuming, but it is time well spent. When you self-publish your manuscript you want it to look professional.

I did say that many writers believe they cannot afford a professional editor. My personal belief is that no author can afford not to hire an editor. Producing a professional looking book is critical to self-publishing. Your book is a product competing with millions of other products out there and it cannot be inferior quality. A poorly edited book – or one that has not been edited at all - is not worth spending a dime on to produce. Plan editing into your budget and you will not regret it.

YOU ARE THE WRITER

Before you publish your book, you have to remember that first you are a writer. You should have worked on perfecting your craft. Writing is not simply a matter of putting words on paper. It takes skill as well as dedication. If you have ever read an interview with a professional writer such as Stephen King, you will be aware that books are not written - they are rewritten. This is such an important point, you should make it into a sign and post it near where you write. My first book was completely rewritten three times. Each time it became a better book. The first edition of this book was rewritten four times. Because I am reworking and updating my material for this second edition, I do not expect to have as many drafts but I will if I think it is necessary. Perfect your craft or you will waste your time self-publishing your material.

You can take courses at your local college or university to learn how to write better. You can subscribe to magazines such as *Writer's Digest* for many how-to articles on various forms of this craft. You can get books at the library. Simply look them up under *Subject: Writing*, take them home and read them. If you find any book that appeals to you, then buy it from a bookstore. The best way to learn about good writing is to read the works of good writers. Find at least three writers who have published in your field. For example, if you have written a regional history, read Pierre Berton's histories. If you are working on a memoir, then read the memoirs or autobiographies of others. When I am working on a book I do not dare get involved in reading a good fiction or I will not get to my computer. What I read for leisure are biographies. The richness of a good biography helps me find ways to convey what I want to say to my readers. A good writer is also an avid reader.

BOOK DESIGN

All books should follow the same design format. They have a front cover, preliminary material (prelims), text, back matter, and a back cover. Each part is an important element in the book. Your book will look very amateurish if you do not follow the accepted format. A frequent problem with self-published books is that the new and unskilled author-publisher does not do enough homework to find out about proper book design. Never forget that your book is competing for shelf space against trade published books designed by professionals from all over the world. Attention to detail is critical.

Another problem with amateurs is believing that their book will stand out if it is somehow different. Unfortunately, booksellers and libraries do not want "different." They want books to have the same elements. If the big publishing houses do not tamper with the accepted design of a book, why on earth would you? It is a death knell for your book if you deviate from accepted industry design.

FRONT COVER

Yes, you can tell a book by its cover these days. Potential readers will first look at the cover to determine if they want to select your book or put it back on the shelf. An unattractive cover will not sell books. Of course an attractive cover will not guarantee sales either, but it will help tremendously. Studies have shown that you have seven seconds to catch the attention of a prospective book purchaser. The cover is also critical in catching the attention of book review editors. A well designed cover is very important.

Unless you are an artist, and have some experience designing books, hire a professional. Cover design is an area where it pays to spend money. Look under *Graphic Designers* in the yellow pages of your telephone book or do a web search. When you make contact, ask if the person has had any experience designing book covers. With those who respond positively, make an appointment to view their previous work. If you do not like what you see, go elsewhere. It is important that you never forget you are running a publishing business now. You have to make business-like decisions about your product. And some business decisions are hard to make. You simply cannot accept inferior packaging for your book. You will benefit from taking the time to find an artist who can produce a cover that will stand up to the competition on a bookstore shelf.

Do not think you will be able to find a good designer only in the large cities. I was able to find an experienced book cover designer in the small town where I live - with a population of less than 5,000. You will be surprised at the array of resource people you can find, even in smaller communities. With internet capability, many artists find they can live in a small community and e-mail or courier their work to customers. No matter where you find him or her, look at their other work first before you sign a contract. And do not hire a graphic designer based solely on how cheaply they work. You get what you pay for and your cover is too important to scrimp on.

BACK COVER

The back of the cover is as important as the front. Although many people simply look at the front cover, many more read the text on the back to see what the book is about. Take this book, for example. Did you look at the back cover to see what you might find inside? When you decide on a cover design, do not expect the artist to write the back cover blurb. That is your job. After all, you are the writer and should know best what is in the book. Spend time and ask others for their feedback. A poorly written back cover might lead a potential reader to believe the writing inside also poor.

Go to the library or a bookstore and look at back covers of books similar to yours. In a notebook, jot down ideas that appeal to you. The text should begin with a short paragraph, tantalizing statement or question that acts as a *hook*. This is a strategy used in magazine and newspaper article writing that "hooks" the reader. Bullets are very popular as a way to list what is inside. Each bullet should have a tightly written short sentence following it. If you need to practice the art of rewriting, this is the place to do it. Make up several sample back covers and get opinions on which one works the best.

Fiction, poetry and memoir do not have bullets, but must have a well written paragraph or two that will entice the reader to want to read the story. It has to tantalize the reader and give enough information to sell the book. This is probably the most difficult writing you will ever do. You have to condense your whole story into no more than two paragraphs. Spend time and effort on this. It will pay off.

If you think it is relevant, put a short biography of yourself on the back cover. It should be no more than three sentences long and tell the reader why you are an expert on the subject. If you are not, it could name any achievements that show why you were the best person to write this book. If you do not think a bio is necessary, then simply do not include it. Do not get caught up in your ego and believe you simply must have your bio on the back cover. Should you have your photo on the back cover? Remember you are unknown and your picture will not sell more books. It is better to keep the back cover simple than overwhelm the reader with a photo and biography about someone who is a stranger to them.

The subject reference also goes on the back cover. This tells librarians and bookstore owners in what section to place your book. You can use one, two, or three subjects. You can see on the back cover of this book it says *REFERENCE/WRITING*. That means it could be shelved in either of those sections in a bookstore or library. I chose Reference because many small bookstores do not have a specific publishing, or even writing, section and I want to make it easier for them to understand where to shelve my book. Check with other books in your genre and make sure you give an accurate subject reference so people can find your book in libraries and bookstore.

The barcode is placed on the bottom right of the back cover. Do not use just an ISBN bar, use an EAN bar. It is what libraries and booksellers expect. Do not get a UPC barcode. It is very expensive and completely unnecessary. I will go into detail about barcodes in the next chapter. Place your book's price under the barcode. Often booksellers want their own price label on the book and this placement works best for them. Yes, you have to cater to what the booksellers want because they are the business that will hopefully put your books on their shelves.

Preliminary pages

The preliminary pages or *prelims* are the pages of a book that you have before the actual text or body begins. They are also referred to as *front matter* and are either numbered with a small Roman numeral or have no page number at all. You can find any or all of the following pages in the prelims:

- Half title page
- Frontispiece, series title, list of contributors or blank page
- Title page
- Legal page with copyright notice, publisher's agencies, printing history, country where printed, ISBN, Cataloguing in Print (CIP)
- Dedication
- Epigraph
- Table of contents
- List of illustrations
- List of tables
- Foreword
- Preface
- Acknowledgments (if not part of preface)
- Introduction (if not part of text)
- List of abbreviations or a chronology

Title pages

Some books begin with a half title page that only has the book's title written on it. There is no subtitle on this page, and it is usually set up very simply. The title is normally set near the top of the page with no other information on the page. This is an optional page. You can use a half title page if it fits into your budget.

The full title page will have the book's full title and subtitle on it, the edition if necessary, author, editor or translator's name, publishing company name and location, and the year of publication. If this is a new edition the number of the edition may appear on this page. It is customary to write *Edited by* or *Translated by John Doe* rather than *John Doe, Editor*. If you have an emblem or colophon (logo) for your publishing company, you would use it on this page.

Both the half title and title pages are on the *recto* or right-hand side of the page. This means you will have a blank *verso* or left-hand page between the two. You can put a frontispiece, series title or list of contributors on this page. Or you can leave it blank.

Most non-fiction books should have a subtitle. That way you can give the book a catchy title and then explain more clearly what it is about in the subtitle. Subtitles are normally done in a different typeface and in a slightly smaller point size. This sets it off from the main title of the book. There is no colon or other punctuation mark to separate the two. Short titles are often done in a larger, bolder type to grab the public's attention. The subtitle can be half that size in either bold or regular type. You have to decide which one looks better with the title. If the title is quite long, use a smaller type. This way it will not look crowded in the space. Try out different looks on a computer until you find the one you like best.

Frontispiece

The verso (left) page facing the title page can either be left blank or it can be used as a *frontispiece*. This is a decorative page that features a halftone (photograph) or line drawing relating to the overall theme of the book. Occasionally a short quote or line from a poem is included with the illustration on the frontispiece. It is not common, but can be done.

If the publisher chooses not to use an illustration in the frontispiece, this page can be used to list other books the author has published, other books in a series if this is part of a series, or other books on the same subject offered by the publisher. This page then becomes an *advertisement page*. If it is used as such, then you should use the same typeface as the book's body text. Make sure the book titles are a little larger than the *Other Books by...* line.

The best way to see how you want to set up your prelims is to go to the library and spend some time looking at books. They do not necessarily have to be about the same subject as yours, but try to keep it to the same genre. For example, if you have written a history, then look at histories and biographies. At the very least look at non-fiction in general. Get a feel for what looks clean and professional, and what looks plain gaudy. Take a notepad and write down things you like about other book's prelims. This will assist you in making your design decisions.

Copyright page

The reverse side (verso) of the title page is the copyright page. The word copyright comes from two familiar words: *copy* and *right*. This page is also known as the *legal page*. Both terms describe it nicely. This page is important because it protects both the author and the publisher from illegal reproduction or other unauthorized use of the contents of the book. You do not want anyone plagiarizing your material. That means they take what you wrote and put their name to it. Just as you should never do this yourself, you do not want others helping themselves to your work and taking credit for it. If anyone wants to quote you, the copyright page will give them information on where to get permission so they can give you credit for your work.

At the top of the page place the copyright symbol © along with the year of publication and your name. You can also use the word *Copyright*. It is not necessary to have both, but most trade publishers still seem to prefer doing that. The symbol alone suits the copyright requirements of North America, most European countries, and many Asian countries. Beside your name print the phrase "All rights reserved". This ensures protection in most Latin American countries.

It is important to use the date the book is actually published. This is not necessarily the same date the book is printed. If the publication date is near the end or beginning of the year, this can be a difficult decision. But as long as the date is no more than one year off, it will not be a problem. A date that is more than a year off will have to be corrected. Pre-planning will help ensure this problem does not crop up.

Often there is a paragraph describing exactly what it is illegal to do with the book. Although not necessary, many publishers prefer to spell out just what a potential plagiarist cannot do and I recommend you do too. This short paragraph ensures no one can claim they did not know exactly what a copyright means. If you want to register the copyright you can do so at **www.cipo.ic.gc.ca**

The website is easy to use and all you have to do is follow the instructions. Copyright is more fully explained in Chapter Three.

If this is not the first printing of your book, you should include the publishing history next. The year of first publication is first on the line, and the current edition is written beside it. To avoid having the printer completely reset this page, some publishers will include a line of consecutive numbers. They are set up left to right ranging from largest to smallest. This way the printer only has to delete the number of the previous edition. Otherwise you will print the edition number completely each time you put out another edition. If your book is realistically only going to be printed once, do not bother with this at all. If by some stroke of luck you get to print several editions of your book, you can use whichever method you prefer.

The name of the country where the book is printed must appear on the copyright page. Some publishers put it before the CIP information and some put it at the bottom of the page. It is a matter of choice. This information must also appear on the back cover or jacket. This way, the book is identified as a Canadian publication. If you have the book printed in another country, it will not be considered a Canadian book. More self-publishers and small subsidies are having book printed offshore. Let me reiterate – it is not considered a Canadian book unless it is printed in Canada.

Some people who have self-published like to give a little free advertising for those who have supported them. You can print the name of the firm who designed the cover or who actually printed the book. Even though you have paid for their services, you might be pleased enough to include this information. In a trade publishing house, these things are done in-house, so they do not normally print it on the legal page. Unfortunately, including the printer's name and cover designer also gives away the fact this is a self-published book. But it is not necessary to list these people on the legal page. You might prefer, instead, to include these people in your acknowledgement.

In order to complete the copyright page, you have to have the CIP information. It is important that the information be placed on the page exactly as you receive it, including proper spacing and punctuation. You need to put the ISBN on this page too. You do have the choice, though, of placing the ISBN either above the CIP information or beneath it.

The name and address of the publisher is printed at the bottom of the page. In trade publishing, the author's personal information is not given to the public - all mail goes through the publisher. Make sure you use the proper mailing address. This way if a reader wants to send a fan letter, they send it to the publisher. If someone wishes to quote from the book, they can request permission by writing to the publisher. If your publishing business address is also your personal address, you have two choices: you can use the address with just the name of your publishing business or you can use a post box number. Be forewarned that using a post box number red flags a self-published book. At the same time, you might be concerned about security. This is one of those business decisions you have to make for yourself.

There are many setups for the copyright page. You can print all the information on the bottom half of the page, the top half of the page, or over the whole page. There is no set industry standard for this and it is simply personal choice. Look at copyright pages in books at the library and use a setup that you personally like. Do not get all hung up on the design of this page. It is the legal page and requires certain information about your book to be included. Keep it simple and clean looking.

Dedication

The first recto page after the title page is where you would place a dedication if you have one. Many authors dedicate their book to a loved one or in the memory of a deceased person or historical figure. This is where you put your author's hat back on and dedicate your book to anyone you choose. It can be short or long. Again this is the author's choice.

The dedication page is usually in the same type and size as the body of the text. You can use any decorative element you want to make it a little fancier, but this is not commonly done. The most decoration you might find is a short dedication written in italics. The dedication is normally centred on the page with the first line about one-third of the way down. You do not sign the dedication because the reader already knows these are the author's words.

Epigraph

Some books contain an *epigraph.* This is a quotation pertinent to the book. As mentioned earlier, if space is at a premium, a short quotation can be put on the frontispiece. But normally it has its own page. If there is no dedication, the epigraph can be put on that page. If costs are getting high, and you really feel the book benefits from an epigraph, you can put it on the blank verso page facing the text or at the beginning of the first chapter.

An epigraph is done in the same text and size as the body, and is usually in italics. The source of the quotation is given on a line following the quotation. It is aligned right with no parentheses or brackets, although it can be preceded by a dash. If the author of the quotation is well known, you simply use the last name. If not, give the author's full name and the title of the work. You do not have to give bibliographical details for an epigraph.

Table of contents

The table of contents, or simply *contents*, is a very important part of the prelims. A potential reader will often open a book to the contents to see exactly what it contains. So you have to remember that this is part of the selling feature of your book. It will do you no good if it is "slapped together." Give the contents a lot of thought and try out different designs. Readers use the contents to find their way around a book. It must be designed for ease of use.

The table of contents always begins on a recto page. It includes chapter numbers and names, and the page each chapter starts on. It also lists the page numbers for back matter such as the index, glossary, and any appendices.

Desktop publishing software can automatically make a table of contents from your manuscript and so can many word processing programs. Make sure there is a good contrast between the different parts of your contents. You may have divided your book into sections or parts as well as chapters. Each element should stand out distinctly from other elements. Never use all the same font type and size to create a table of contents. This not only shows your lack of experience, but it is difficult for a reader to use. Too often self-published books have a table of contents that has the chapter name, a row of dots, and the page number. It is neither good looking nor useful. Like other parts of book design, look at books in the library for models you like.

Lists

If you have written a technical manual or serious historical book, you might have several illustrations or tables you need to include. The easiest way for the reader to find them, or keep track of them, is to list them separately. Lists are optional, but if you decide to include them you want to do them accurately.

The list of illustrations comes first. It is titled simply *Illustrations*. The size and type of fonts should match the table of contents. It may be divided into sections such as Figures, Maps, etc. The title you give the illustration in the list does not have to be exactly the same title used for the actual illustration. It can be a simplified version. Normally, sections of photographs like you would find in a history book are not given in a list of illustrations. Sometimes your illustrations are inserted after the book is made up into pages and will not have a page number. When this happens you list it as *facing page 00* or *following page 00*. This enables the reader to find the nearest numbered page and look at the illustration.

The list of tables is placed next. If there

is no list of illustrations, then the tables page is placed after the contents. Labeled *Tables*, it shows readers where they can find tables, charts, or graphs. Rules for design and numbering are the same as I have just detailed for illustrations.

Foreword

Try not to mistake a book *foreword* for the direction of forward. The one used in publishing is made up of two words - *fore*: first or in front of, and *word*: text. In order to make sure you do not misspell it, try to remember it is as the "first word". Which in effect, it is. It is an introductory statement written by someone other than the author. It can be a well known person or someone who knows about the subject of the book. It can be a few paragraphs long or can run into several pages. Regardless of length, it is done in the same typeface as the text of the book. The writer's name is placed at the end, often in caps and small caps, and it is aligned with the right margin. If the foreword is quite long, the writer's name may be given at the beginning instead of the end. Although many trade publishers include the place (institution or city) and the date, some style books discourage this practice. If you do choose to include it, this information is set flush left with a line between it and the text of the foreword.

Finding someone to write the foreword can be a bit of a challenge. You would normally write a letter to the person you want to write it and ask if they are willing. You should include a copy of the galleys if they are ready, or at least a copy of the manuscript. A person well known in a particular field will want to see the book before putting their name in it. A famous person will be hard to both track down and pin down. They get many requests for favours such as this. Do not let anyone charge you a fee for writing a foreword.

Having a foreword written can be an exercise in diplomacy. Sometimes the writer will do a great job. Other times you have to edit the text. And there are even times when you will be asked to write the foreword yourself for the writer's approval and name. Ideally you should give the writer a clear idea why you chose them. In a book about the history of a Sea Cadet summer training centre, I asked a retired Admiral to write the foreword because I knew he had been there as a young teenager and that he returned for his retirement parade. I saw it as a full circle and wanted him to write along that vein. It took several drafts to get it, but it did require a lot of diplomacy to deal with editing and rewriting. This is something experienced publishers deal with all the time, so try to think about how they would handle it. This is the time when you put on your business hat.

If you think a foreword would enhance your book, look at other sources. It could be someone local who is knowledgeable about the subject. It could be someone you know who can tell why the book would be important to read. If you cannot find someone to write a foreword, leave it out. Instead you can write a preface.

Preface

The preface is written to explain to the reader why or how the author wrote the book. It can include the method of research if it is important, permission for using previously published material, and acknowledgements. It should be kept fairly short - no more than one page. It is not necessary to have your name here because the reader will presume it was written by the author whose name appears on the title page, especially as it will be written in the first person. If the list of people you want to thank is relatively short, they can be included in the preface.

Acknowledgement

If there is no preface, or if the list of people who helped get the book published is too long, a separate page for acknowledgements is inserted. If the preface consists of little more than thank-you notes, an acknowledgement page would be used instead of a preface page.

As with the introduction, foreword, and preface, the acknowledgement page should be set up in the same type and size as the text in the body. The headings for these pages are normally done in a bolder type and can be one size larger. This is your choice. You can look at prelims in books in the library to see what you like. You can also try out different styles on the computer. Make sure you print out a hard copy so you get an accurate idea of what it looks like.

Introduction

In some kinds of books an introduction is necessary to provide background information. Material that is relevant to the book and needs to be read before the text, should not be put into the preface, but written in the introduction. This may be written by the author or another person with expertise on the topic.

If the introduction is a prelim, it is to be numbered in lower case Roman numerals. If it is going to be part of the text, it is numbered in Arabic numerals. If it is used to set the scene for the book, it should be considered part of the text.

Often writers confuse the *introduction* and the *preface*. Make sure you understand what each is and label them correctly. To do otherwise will indicate you are an amateur.

List of abbreviations

In technical books and some how-to books there might be a lot of unusual terms, abbreviations or acronyms for the reader to grasp. In this case, you might want to include a list of abbreviations and explanations. If the list is one page it is placed on the verso page immediately before the text begins. If it is longer than a page, put this section in the book's back matter. Abbreviations are always listed in alphabetical order.

Editorial method

Scholarly books often include an explanation of the approach the author or editor has taken to the subject matter. If it is long, include it as a separate section. If it is short, and merely points out things such as word spelling or modernization of grammar, it should be included in the Preface.

List of contributors

When the book has contributions from several authors, you will include a list of contributors. It is most commonly set up in alphabetical order by author's surname. Their position or credentials are listed under their name. Sometimes a short biography is included.

Chronology

Historical books or novels have many characters and/or time periods in them. The best way to give the reader a clear understanding of events and characters as they appear is to include a chronology, designed so that the date is located along the left margin. The information is either placed at the right of the date or beneath it. It is best to put the chronology right before the text begins so it is easy to refer to. You can, though, put it after the text in the back matter. You also have the choice of having the whole chronology in the same type or making the dates bold. You have to decide which works best for your book.

BODY OF THE BOOK

The preliminary pages should serve as a guide to the contents and nature of a book. The back matter provides reference material. Sandwiched in between is the *text*. Although not as extensive to design as prelims or back matter, it is the most important part of a book. It is, in fact, the book itself. Beginning as your idea, then created as a manuscript, the text is the body and soul of your book. We have already discussed the importance of producing your best writing, and having it carefully edited. Now you want to set it up to help, not hinder, the reader.

In book design, font is called *typeface*. Do not be confused by the term. All they mean is the type of letters that will be used for the book. When writing for print, use a serif typeface and when writing for an e-book or website, use a sans serif typeface. This will be explained in more detail in a later chapter.

Chapters

Text is normally divided into *chapters*. You should already know where your chapter breaks are going to be. Although they do not have to be exactly the same length, they should also not be too noticeably different in size. Chapter titles should be fairly short and give a reasonable idea as to what is in the chapter. Remember, the chapter titles are what you use to make up your table of contents. Many potential book buyers check out the contents to see what the book is about. If your chapter titles are vague or cute, they will not convey the book's contents very well and you could lose potential sales.

Each chapter starts on a new page, preferably a recto page. If you can afford the extra few pages, it should ideally start on a recto page. But it is equally acceptable these days for a chapter to start on a verso page. A chapter has a *heading* also called the *chapter display*. It may include the chapter number, title, an epigraph (quote), and an author's name if this chapter was written by a different author. The chapter number can be centred, aligned left, or aligned right. It can be an actual number or the number written out. If you plan to write it out, make sure the page does not get too cluttered with the title. The chapter heading is normally set in a larger type style. The text of the chapter does not begin until part way down the page - at least a third of the way down is usually acceptable. Make sure all your chapter headings have exactly the same font, size, and alignment.

Occasionally a book will be divided into *parts*. This is most commonly found in historical fiction, multiple volume science fiction, or novels that encompass a large time span. Parts are also used in technical books, scholarly books, and large scale non-fiction books. It is recommended that the novice stay away from too many divisions, but use them if necessary to best organize your book. They should be designed to match chapter headings. The type of numbering should be identical as well as the font, size and alignment. You might notice during your research trips to the library or bookstore that some part headings look different than the chapter headings. Unless you have experience in using complimentary fonts, I do not recommend you try this. Stay with a simple, visually acceptable format. Take time to write the title for each part as you do for chapter headings. These too will be included in your table of contents.

Headings

In many non-fiction books, *headings* and *subheadings* are used to break the material into manageable lengths. You can see that I have done that in this book. It helps the reader find material more quickly. The chapter heading is a *major head* done in large, bold type style. A heading is a *minor head* done in a type style that is larger than the one you are using for the text of the book, but smaller than the chapter heading. Subheads tend to be a bold version of the text you are using. Do not get too carried away with heads and subheads or it will detract from the main message of the book. Make sure they are sufficiently distributed. If one chapter has several heads and the next only has one, it will look awful. It would be better to rethink the use of headings altogether. Do not use sans serif heads with serif type.

At the top of every page in the book you will find *running heads*. They were named because they run across the top margin of the page. They can be used to identify the book title, chapter title, or section title. And I have even seen some that have the author's name. You have to decide which title you want to put in your running head. The most common two are either the book title on the verso page and the chapter title on the recto page, or the chapter title on all pages in that chapter. Again it is personal choice and is something you should look at on your trips to the library or bookstore when you research book design.

I have seen books that have the running head on the bottom of the page. Trade publishers do not do it, so you should not do it either. Page numbers can go on the bottom of the page, but not running heads. Do not let an inexperienced designer convince you to try it either. It is not acceptable book design.

Epilogues and Afterwords

Part of the text, an *epilogue* or *afterword* allows the author to have a final word with the reader. It may encourage readers to find out more about the topic or pursue goals the book has presented. It may give the reader information on other books covering the same topic, although this can be accomplished with a list in the back matter. In fiction, an epilogue is often used to let the reader know where the characters are in a later time frame. Whether you decide to use them or not, epilogues and afterwords should be kept brief.

An author who wants to sum up the book topic would write a *conclusion*. More common in academic books, a conclusion can be fairly extensive and could take up as many pages as an actual chapter of the book. In some types of non-fiction books, the conclusion is actually quite detailed.

BACK MATTER

The *back matter* of a book acts as a reference section for the reader. This is where you put information that would help your reader to understand the text, but which was not really right for the text. Back matter may be made up of any of the following:

- Appendix
- Glossary
- Bibliography
- Index

Just because these sections are located at the back of the book does not mean they are not an important part of book design. They must be planned as carefully as prelims and text. Back matter is set in the same type style as the text, and can numbered in Arabic numerals.

Appendix

An *appendix* is a section, or several sections, of a book that can give the reader data, explanations, elaborations, texts of documents, laws, survey questions and results, or long lists. The appendixes in this book mostly give lists of websites. You can refer to them when you want the information, but I have not cluttered the text up with long lists of websites. The appendixes are done in a smaller type style.

You may think the plural *appendixes* is wrong, and that it should be *appendices*. According to the Webster's Universal Dictionary, they are both correct. You decide which term you want to use.

Glossary

The *glossary* is an alphabetical listing of terms used throughout the book, along with their definitions. It is commonly found in books that use unique or technical words. Because you may not be familiar with publishing or its terminology, I have included a glossary in the back matter of this book. Although you can define terms as they appear in the text, remember that back matter is used as reference. The reader can refer to the glossary later instead of looking up words in the text .

Each word or phrase is printed in boldface type. Sometimes it is italicized too. The first letter can be capitalized or the whole term can be in lowercase letters. It is important to remember that each definition in the glossary ends with a period, even if it is not a proper sentence. The text is all flush left with the margin. This means there are no indentations.

Bibliography

If you use other books or articles while

researching your book, you should include a *bibliography*. A single list of sources is most commonly presented in alphabetical order. A lengthy list, or one from several sources, can be separated into sections by subject or kinds of material.

There are many acceptable format styles to choose from. The most common one is the *flush and hang* style. This means that the first line of each entry is flush with the left margin while the rest of the entry is indented (or hangs). I personally prefer to use *The Chicago Manual of Style* as my model for style decisions. Whichever style guide you decide to use, be consistent. Decide on the style guide you prefer and stick with it.

Index

A non-fiction book will be harder to sell without an *index*. Booksellers and librarians will look for one, and may not order your book if it does not have an index. It is the main reference that you provide for your readers when they need to find something quickly. Spend the time to do it right.

All pertinent words, phrases and names are included in the index. It is organized in alphabetical order by the first word. If the first word is *a, an* or *the*, you organize that phrase or title alphabetically by the second word. New word processing and desktop publishing software can do the job for you. Take a look at specific editing software on the market. If you do not have access to a computer, write each word or name on a separate index card and then put them in alphabetical order. As you set up the index, try to imagine what a reader might want to look up. When you are finished, look carefully at your list to make sure you chose important words. Do not make the index too long or too brief. You might want to ask someone to read the manuscript and make suggestions about concepts they find that need inclusion in the index. If you can afford it, consider hiring a freelancer to make up your indexes. Provide a copy of the typeset manuscript for them to work from so they know what pages each term falls on.

Colophon

What is a colophon? It is information at the very end of a book giving the reader a description of the text typography. It was used in ancient Egyptian and Roman times to identify who wrote the script and who commissioned it. A colophon is normally titled *A note about the type* and will identify the names of the primary typefaces used and provide a brief statement about its most identifiable physical characteristics. It may also identify the book's designer, software used, printing method, the printing company, and the kind of ink, paper and its cotton content. A colophon is not normally used in this day and age unless you are writing an academic book, limited edition or private press printing.

Order form

You will never find an order form in a book published by the trade book industry. The industry presumes if you want a copy of the book, you know enough to go to a bookstore and look for it or order it online. If you have to have it ordered, you give the bookstore the name of the book and the author, if you know it, and they will order it for you. If you include an order form at the back, or even ordering information, it will be immediately apparent the book is self-published.

That said, it could help your sales to have an order form on the very last page of the book. David Chilton (*The Wealthy Barber*) was convinced to do this by a well known self-publishing consultant. The sales of his already successful book increased noticeably. Since the crash of the economy in 2008, many of the rules in publishing are changing. If you have a great book that is well designed, there should be no reason to hide the fact that it is self-published. Most books on self-publishing recommend that mail order information should be included. This is one of those publishing decisions I mention periodically throughout this book. Decide what works best for your book.

If you choose to have an order form, it should be placed on the recto side of the last page in the book. Do not have it on the verso side of a page with text. This gives the reader a dilemma as to whether they want to cut up their book. I realize it could be photocopied, but as the publisher you want to make it as easy as possible for copies of your book to be ordered.

SUMMARY

Now you know how to choose a subject, edit the manuscript, and design a book. Sounds easy when I put it this way. But doing the work is not easy. It requires attention to detail and several trips to the library or a bookstore to do research. The goal is to give your book the most professional look you can achieve. To be successful, you have to think professionally. You do not have the luxury of sending the book to different in-house departments like a trade publishing house does. You are all those departments! Whenever you can afford to hire an expert, do so. It will make your job less painful. Before you make a design decision, ask yourself if it is going to help your book look more professional. Never forget, your book competes against professionally produced ones. Be prepared to spend the time, and the money if you have to, in order to give the competition a run for their money.

CHAPTER THREE

Make It Legal

A book is as individual as a fingerprint
— Sylvia Fraser

GETTING READY

Now that you have a manuscript, and know how you want both the outside and inside of your book to be designed, you need to get ready for the printer. Surprisingly, you have a lot of paperwork to fill out before you get to that stage. You cannot have the manuscript formatted until you complete the following steps. While you may sigh and wonder what all this has to do with self-publishing, you need to understand this chapter because it is integral to the publication of a saleable book. Without it, your chances of sales may drop to virtually zero.

Copyright

One of the first things new authors often ask is about how to copyright their material. As I said in Chapter Two, it is not necessary to register the copyright in order to have protection in Canada. Many authors want to register their book, though, because they want the certificate that is issued. The certificate is evidence that your work is protected by copyright and you are the legal owner. Some authors think you should do it as a matter of course. Others believe that if your work is available only in Canada or in your province, or even your local community, that the expenditure is unnecessary. Like many aspects of publishing, this is a personal decision.

When you decide to register copyright of your book, you will also want to make sure you keep proof of your work. This is done so that your claim of original work has something to back it up. If there is ever a dispute about who created the work, it may end up in court. You will need evidence from those who saw the work in progress as well as previous drafts of your work. Some of the evidential items you might want to have would include the following:

- Dated drafts and outlines
- Dated research records used to create the work
- Names of those you shared the work

with at different stages
- Written records of any agreements made concerning creation of material or ownership of copyright material

Mailing a registered copy of the manuscript to yourself is not sufficient proof that the work is yours. Do not let anyone tell you it is okay because it is not. It has been tested in a court of law and has not held up. This method does not satisfy the requirement that you wrote the manuscript. Save your money and follow the methods of proof that I have already outlined.

The Canadian Copyright Office is handled by the federal government Intellectual Property Office. You can register either online, by fax or via regular post. The form is on the website at **www.cipo.ic.gc.ca** The time it takes to register your copyright depends on whether any revisions or corrections are required, but normally it would be five business days for filing. Under normal circumstances, you should receive your registration certificate within four to six weeks from the time the Copyright Office receives it. Make sure you plan copyright registration into your timetable.

Cost of copyright at time of printing is $50.00 if you pay online and $65.00 if you make payment another way. In other words, you pay extra for the processing. There are fees for corrections and fees for duplicates. Read the Fees section of the website carefully so there are no surprises.

When you Google *Canadian copyright registration*, you will see that the Business Development Bank of Canada (BDBC) is also registering copyright. They register it for you, but you pay for the service. There are currently three price packages for registering copyright – Basic, Standard and Professional Copyright Registrations Packages. Each one comes with a different price tag. At time of printing the cost of the Basic Package was nearly $120.00 which includes the BDBC fee, the actual filing fee, shipping and handling, and of course taxes.

ISBN

The International Standard Book Number (ISBN) identifies your book as a unique publication around the world. Each book, as well as each edition of a book, has its own ISBN. There might be other books in the world with the same title or another author with the same name as you, but the ISBN is unique. The thirteen-digit number allows booksellers to order books accurately and efficiently. Since computers are so commonly used in business, the ISBN has become essential. Most booksellers use some kind of database program, and books are entered by their ISBN rather than their title.

The ISBN for this book is 978-1-894208-00-0. The "978" is the new thirteen digit ISBN.

The "0" or a "1" shows that the book originated in an English speaking country. For international purposes, Canada is considered to be English speaking. The block of six numbers identifies the publisher. In this case it identifies my company, Half Acre Publishing. The "00" tells us what title and edition of the book we are looking at and identifies it as a hardcover or softcover edition. In our example, this is the second softcover edition. The last number is a check digit - a mathematical function to make sure the rest of the numbers are correct. It ensures they have not been miscopied.

You order the ISBN from the National Library of Canada **www.collectionscanada. gc.ca**. Unlike the United States, there is no charge for ISBN in Canada. You can only order individually unless you are a major publisher. At one time we could order blocks of 10 or 100, but that is no longer allowed. The form is online and is self-explanatory. Make sure you have your ISBN before your books are printed.

In order to be considered self-published, you are required to have your own ISBN. Being issued with a number from another publisher can cause unexpected problems. When I self-published my first book, the printer issued me with an ISBN from his block of numbers. Several orders went to his place of business because the publisher identification number is his, not mine. On one occasion a cheque for my book, made out in his company's name, was even mailed to him. We both had some bookkeeping to fix up after that. If someone offers to "issue you with an ISBN" I recommend you politely refuse. Otherwise the book industry will consider that person to be the publisher. If it is someone you know well, or you would prefer not to have orders come to your home, then by all means accept an issued ISBN. Make sure you keep in contact with the person or company who issues the ISBN to you or you could miss out on orders or payments.

Subsidy and POD publishers often insist on issuing you with an ISBN. That means they are considered to be the publisher, not you. You cannot call yourself a self-publisher if your book is published by someone else. Reviewers will not even look at your book if it has the imprint of someone other than yourself. If the publisher moves or goes out of business, you will not know what has happened to your book orders. You are paying for your book and you are entitled to have your own little publishing company name on it. Of course, if you only want a small print run, and do not care if it will be sold, then accept an issued ISBN.

CIP

Cataloguing in Publication (CIP) is a voluntary program that catalogues Canadian books nationally and internationally before they are published. This cataloguing information is distributed right away to librarians and booksellers. It allows librarians, wholesalers, and booksellers to select and purchase new Canadian books. It is voluntary, does not cost any money, and is a great way to get your book introduced in the marketplace. Since it is used by the trade publishers, your book will look more professional having a CIP.

You apply online at the National Library's website at **www.collectionscanada.gc.ca**. It is a matter of filling in the blanks on the form. If the book has an introduction, preface, and table of contents, it can be attached to the form. You might want to write down where these files are on your computer before you begin. The turnaround is quick so as not to hold up publishing schedules. They will not issue a CIP in less than ten business days, so make sure you plan that into your publishing schedule. If you need it rushed, you will need a very good reason - and poor planning is not a good reason. Before you submit it, though, you must make sure you know what subjects your book should be listed under and you must already have your ISBN number. If you have organized the publishing of your book properly, you will have your CIP in plenty of time to put the information on your copyright page before it goes for formatting. Make sure you place it on the page <u>exactly</u> the way it is sent to you. This is important. If you cannot import it into your formatting program and have to copy it, check it three times to ensure it has been input correctly.

New Book Service

The National Library has a program called *New Book Service* that assists publishers to promote their books. The form is also online just below the CIP form. You can include graphics and promotional text with this form. Some of the promotional material can include the foreword, a sample chapter, reviews, awards won, and information about readings. You can either e-mail it with the attachments or you can print and mail or FAX this information. You will require a JPG or GIF graphic file of your book's cover. It has to be no larger than 72 pixels per inch and the longest side cannot be larger than nine inches. You can use a PDF file for the text. Make sure the whole package is no larger than 200 kilobytes. The service is a free of charge and can be very beneficial to any publisher, but especially useful for small self-publishers. It is worth taking the time to submit your listing to the New Book Service.

BOWKERLINK

The R.R. Bowker Data Collection Centre is an American company that puts out several important directories a year, including *Books in Print*. Even though this is not a Canadian directory, it is used by booksellers throughout North America. There is no fee to register your publishing company and books.

In order to have your book listed, you have to use the BowkerLink Publisher Access System at **www.bowkerlink.com**. You need to register both your book and your publishing company. Follow all instructions and your username and password will be e-mailed back to you to be validated. This might take up to three business days.

Although Bowkerlink prefers to receive bibliographic information online, you can still use the old fashioned fill-out-the-form method. The Advance Book Information form is commonly called the ABI in the industry. It is easy to fill out and includes a guide explaining what each line requires. Order one from Bowkerlink well in advance of your book's print date. Note that this is for *advance* information. But do not panic if you are under a tight deadline. You can still send in the ABI to be included in the Canadian edition.

After you have filled out the form, make several photocopies. You can include them in your media packages that we will discuss in Chapter Six. The information required on the form gives details about your book. Any distributor, publicist, or reviewer will be grateful for that. It will also give your book a better chance at being read by these people.

R.R. Bowker
630 Central Ave
New Providence, NJ
USA 07974

Do not forget to use enough postage on the envelope to send it to the United States or it will be returned to you.

LEGAL DEPOSIT

Since 1953, when the National Library of Canada was created, Legal Deposit has been in effect to ensure books are "accessible to present and future generations." A depository of all new Canadian books, the National Library administers legal deposit as part of its responsibility to preserve Canada's heritage of published works.

Each Canadian publisher is required to send copies within one week after the book's release. How many you send depends on how many you produce. If you make 101 or more copies of your book, you must send two copies to the National Library. If you make more than three and less than 101 copies, you are only required to send one copy. If you publish less than three copies, you do not have to send anything. Copies of books sent to legal deposit are a deductible expense on your taxes, as well the postage paid for sending them.

Publications received by legal deposit

are catalogued and listed in *Canadiana*, the national bibliography which is circulated in Canada and other countries. Sometimes the books are the subject of public readings and author book signings as part of the National Library's public program events. When you bundle up your book(s) to send, there is a form to include. You can request it when you order your ISBN and CIP from the National Library.

BAR CODES

If you turn this book over you will see a bar code on the back cover. It is used to identify this book when retailers run it past their scanners at the cash register. These are the days of technology, and this is how retailers keep records of products and prices.

The most common bar code found on books is the *Bookland EAN* code. This conforms to the European Article Numbering system. The EAN numbers are at the bottom of the block. The *9 78* means this product is a book. The rest of the number is the book's ISBN number with a different last digit (the check digit). Sometimes the ISBN is also listed at the top of the block. The EAN bar code is used in bookstores only, including the large chain stores. A digital version will cost in the $20 to $35 range.

You have the option of ordering an EAN bar code with an add-on block that is smaller than the EAN bar code and is situated to the right of it. This add-on can be coded with the book's price. When you order your bar code, discuss your needs with the company you order it from. Bar codes can be put on the book by your designer. A good designer has the software to do this. Otherwise Goggle bar codes on the internet. You can use barcode software if you feel comfortable with it. You can find software on the internet. It should cost no more than having a company make it though, so you might as well have someone else do it. Oddly, the software prints barcode labels. I would recommend if you want the code printed directly on your book cover, have it made professionally by your designer.

The type of bar code you might be most familiar with is the Universal Product Code or UPC. This block is on pretty well everything we purchase these days. You do not need to purchase a UPC bar code. If a department store or grocery chain plans to sell your book, they will look after any UPC labels if it becomes necessary. They are very expensive so do not waste your money.

The bar code goes on the lower right side or centre of the back cover of a softcover book. If you are publishing a hardcover book, it should be placed on the top of the left hand flap of the dust cover. If you are still unsure where to place it, go to the library or bookstore and have a look at books there. Correct placement of the bar code is another way to make your book look professional. If you have any questions, do not hesitate to ask experienced distributors or trade publishers. And if you have printed a book without a bar code, you can still order packages of stickers. Mind you, it is quite a chore to attach 500 or 1,000 stickers to your books, so you want to make sure you plan ahead.

PRICING THE BOOK

At this time you have to decide on the cost of your book to the consumer. You will be asked for this information on many of the previously discussed forms. It is a fairly tough decision. You want to price it so you make money from the book, but ensure the price is not so high that no one will want to buy it. You want to make sure you are making a reasonable profit from your business venture or you will not feel encouraged to do it again. There is no reason why you should have to support your self-publishing like it was a hobby. You might not make a lot of money, but you should at least make enough to pay for the product and your time.

Interestingly, if you price a book too low you actually harm your chances of selling many books. In the publishing industry there is a fair market value put on books. This price is determined by several factors such as size, length, and product cost, among other things. If you price your book too low, potential readers might wonder what is wrong with it. You also cut into your profit. This profit is necessary to promote and publicize your book. If you do not have enough money to do this, you will see sales dry up. Too many new author-publishers price their book too low, thinking it will sell more quickly. Do not forget that book purchasers are shrewd consumers. They love books, are willing to pay a reasonable amount for books, and know what books are worth. Do not insult the intelligence of your potential buyers. You are the one who will suffer in the end.

So just how does one actually price a book? The obvious answer is to figure out the production cost and multiply it by the industry standard for pricing. There is a set industry standard which most self-publishers know nothing about. Of the three best books on self-publishing I found recommendations for pricing as varied as "4-5 times", "5-8 times", and "not less than 8" times the production cost. One author even suggested that mail order how-to books run 10-20 times production cost. How is that for variation? In Canada, trade publishers use a formula to determine the cost of a book:

F (fixed cost) + V (variable cost) = Production cost
Production cost / Print run = Unit cost
Unit cost x cost factor (4,5,6) = Cover price

So how do you figure this out? Fixed costs remain the same no matter how many books you print and can include editing, cover design and typesetting. Variable costs are those that change with the size of the print run and can include paper, printing costs, and cost of binding. You add these costs up and divide that amount by the number of books you plan to produce. This gives you the exact cost of producing each book or *unit cost*. Canadian publishers multiply the unit cost by either 4, 5, or 6 to get their *markup*. So how do you know which factor to use to determine the markup of your book?

The first thing you have to determine is the number of pages in the printed book. The total page count includes prelim and back matter. Your print costs will also be strongly influenced by total page count. Go to your favourite bookstore and find books with the same (or close to) page count, same number of colours on the cover (two or four), and similar subject matter. This will give you a ballpark idea of the minimum price that books like yours are selling for.

The next step is to figure out the expenses involved with producing your book. You want to include editing, typesetting, design, cover, and printing costs as well as advertising and marketing costs. If you do not have all these costs figured out yet, now is the time to do it. You will need to get printer's estimates and decide which one you plan to accept. When the time comes to set the price for your book, you have to put on your "business hat" and pull all the information together to make an informed decision. After you have calculated all costs involved in the production of the book, divide the total by the number of books you intend to print (the print run) to reach the unit cost. Then multiply that number by 5 (the markup). See how it stacks up against the books you have looked at in the bookstore. Decide if you have to adjust the price lower or higher. If it is within a dollar of other books, you should be okay. Unless you are planning to specialize in educational publishing where the mark up is usually 8, you should use 4, 5, or 6 as your markup number.

Do not choose a price that is an even amount. The "rule of .99" is the rule of consumerism. If your book is worth about $15.00, price it at $14.99. Even though consumers are more savvy today, many studies show that this strategy still works. At one time it was advised to use an even number for the price if you were marketing solely by mail order, but with so much online sales these days you need to price the product the way you would for a real shelf.

When you total up the cost to produce your book and you find you can only charge two or three times the cost, you have to go back to the drawing board for some more hard decisions. If your printer's estimates are not too similar, you might want to go with a less expensive printer. Perhaps you can shorten the page count. This is done by either doing some serious editing or making the font size and leading smaller. Another way is to use cheaper paper, take out some illustrations (especially photographs), or change the colour count for the cover from four to two. This exercise will give you a greater appreciation for trade publishers who have to do this kind of thing all the time. If you cannot make money with an industry mark up, you need to rethink the whole project. Booksellers know the value of books and will not buy something too high-priced to sell.

PUTTING IT ALL TOGETHER

Once you have collected all the information you need, it is time to have your book formatted. Although I go into this in more detail in the next chapter, you need to be careful about where you place such information as the CIP in the book. If you hire someone to format for you, they will have their preference. Make sure it synchronizes with your preferences. You should now be carrying the idea in your head of how you want your book to look.

As you can see, a lot of information is required before you can even have your manuscript turned into a galley. During this process you have to remember to think like a business person. Unless you have to edit for length, the writer part of you must be tucked away. You are now on the track to becoming a self-publisher and have to keep that in mind at all times. If you are still a bit emotionally too connected to your manuscript, perhaps you should put it away for six months and wait until you feel ready to view it in a businesslike manner. Write something else to get it out of your head. Then take it out when you feel you can publish it less emotionally and are ready to view it as a commodity to be sold.

Never lose sight of the fact that you want your book to be professional in appearance so it can compete for shelf space with other publishers. You will need to distance yourself from your book as something that you poured your soul into. You need to think of it as a product to be sold. If any of you have had experience selling anything in your lifetime, you know you sometimes have to make tough decisions in order to make a sale. It is no different in the publishing industry.

CHAPTER FOUR

Building a Book

The purpose of art is the lifelong
construction of a state of wonder.
— Glenn Gould

TYPESETTING

Typesetting is an old publisher's technical term for *formatting* your manuscript. Before computers were invented, individual letter forms made of lead had to be set by hand before a book could be printed. Today this is done on the computer and either printed out for offset printing or saved to a disk for digital printing. Whichever type of printing you choose, your book interior has to be properly designed in order to look like a book. A complete description of everything that should appear between the covers of a book was given in Chapter Two.

In this chapter you will learn the technical specifications for designing a book interior.

Right now your manuscript is probably on 8 ½ x 11 paper (and preferably double spaced). But it could be handwritten or even single spaced. If you have done it on a computer, the next step will be easier to accomplish. What you need to do now is have your manuscript formatted so it looks like a book. This is optimally done with a desktop publishing program like PageMaker or Quark Express or InDesign. While you can technically format your manuscript in a good word processing program, it is better to use DTP software.

And I recommend you never format as you write your book. Since all good books are rewritten rather than written, formatting as you write would require a tremendous number of technical changes each time you make written changes, eating up a lot of time. Write first, and format after it is completed and edited. Another problem to formatting in a word processing program, is the tendency of text blocks to move when you work with them. They do not do that in most DTP software.

YOU OR AN EXPERT

Another big decision you have to make is who will typeset your book. In order to answer this question, you need to answer some important questions:

1. Do you know how to format on your computer using your word processing program?
2. Are you skilled in the use of a good desktop publishing program?
3. Do you know how to make an index on your computer?
4. Do you know the elements of design of the interior of a book?

In Chapter Two, I described all the parts of a book's interior. How well did you understand it? Do you have an eye for design? If you are uncertain, you need to take your manuscript to someone who can format for you. Usually it will be a desktop publishing firm or typesetter. As with other resources that you will do business with, make sure the firm has experience with books. And look at samples of their work. Some firms may have done several books, but not very well. They have a sort of "template" they use and that is what you get. Ask for two or three proofs and do not accept anything less than a professional job. Take a book, either from the library or one you have purchased, and show the firm exactly what you want. There is no copyright on interior book design so you can copy a design feature you like. It will cost you to have someone professional format your book but, like editing, this is some of the best money you will spend on making your book ready for the reading public.

DOING IT YOURSELF

If you plan to do the typesetting yourself, you need to be aware of a few industry standards. Margins are something most self-publishers do not pay attention to. Unfortunately for them, the white space is as important as the text. The page has to be "pleasing to the eye", so to speak. If there is too little white space, it can actually cause anxiety to the reader. This is part of the psychology of reading. I will not go into detail on that here. Just suffice it to say that in the industry white space should account for close to 50% of the book. Art books and highly designed books may have as much as 75% white space. You can save money by having smaller margins, but you may lose money in the long run when your book with the crowded text does not sell. Remember, all money is made from the finished product.

You want to arrange the text on facing pages so it is seen as a unit. Book margins are similar to magazine margins. The narrowest margin on the page is the gutter. At the same time, the combined gutter of both pages is wider than the other margins. The margin at the top of the page is larger, increasing more on the outside edge, and increasing the most on the bottom of the page. A good rule of thumb is to make each margin larger than the other. Make sure the gutter margin is large enough so that the text does not disappear when the book is bound. If you are trying to keep page count down, it is better to adjust font and leading size than be too cheap with the margins.

TYPOGRAPHY

The title page and the first page of each chapter are your showpieces. Make sure they are placed on the recto side of the page. Some publishers are spreading the title across both pages. While this can be dramatic, be careful that it looks that way and not just silly. Typeface (or font) for the chapter headings is normally the same typeface used for the text. You also have to decide how you want to begin your chapter. Some books have a fancy initial letter, which can be in a different font. Some do not indent the first paragraph of the chapter while others indent halfway across the page. You might want to start the chapter a third or even half-way down the page. Decide what looks best for your book.

While headings should be larger than the text, they should be no larger than 18 to 24 points. A small size heading surrounded by white space can be as dramatic as a large size heading. Subheads should be close in size to the text. To distinguish them, try putting them in all caps, bold face or italics. Also try to keep headings from being too close to the bottom of the page and make sure there are no less than three lines of text below a subhead. At the same time, try to have at least two lines above a subhead at the top of a page. These are called widows and orphans and are defined in the Glossary.

How you want running heads or titles and page numbers to appear is another exercise in decision making. You want to make it easy for the reader to always be aware of the book's title, the chapter title, and the page number. In non-fiction, the book title traditionally goes on the left hand page while the chapter title goes on the right. I chose this method, but could have just as easily had the chapter name on both pages, or the book title on both pages. It was my decision. Fiction books normally have either the book title or the chapter title on both pages of the running head. There is no requirement for a line unless you think it benefits the interior design of your book. We used .5 size lines for the running head. And remember that you may not see running heads or titles in a fiction book. Sometimes the author's name is placed there, but I would suggest you leave it out unless you are famous. While it does not matter if your page number is at the top or bottom of the page, I suggest that you put it in the outside margin of the page. If it is a small book, such as a poetry chapbook, you can centre it on the bottom of the page. Page numbers will detract from the text if they are centred on the top of the page.

Do not use a print size smaller than

10 point. If a book is long and you want to keep the page count down, smaller type size might be your only option but do not make it too small. On the other hand, if your book is shorter than you would like, use a larger typeface and more leading (the space between the lines). This book was set at 12 point Bookman with 15 point leading. Make sure your leading is no more than 1 to 3 points different in size than the typeface size. Space between words is usually 1/4 em and no more than 1/3 em. You want your readers to enjoy reading your book and not feel overwhelmed by either too much text or too small sized text on a page. Set your justification at *full* so the text fits nicely between the margins. A decent desktop publishing program will hyphenate automatically.

FONT (TYPEFACE)

The font is the type of letters you use to write your text. There are two major subdivisions in font type: *serif* and *sans serif.* The main feature of a serif font is the cross strokes at the linne ending of each letter. Some people think serif fonts Times New Roman on your computer have little "tails" on some letters. A sans serif font like Arial has no cross strokes. Serif fonts are generally considered to be more readable than sans serif fonts. As already noted, the text in this book is Bookman.

Many types of serif fonts are used in book design. The most commonly used fonts in the Canadian publishing industry are Baskerville, Bodoni, Century, Garamond and Times Roman. You should be familiar with the latter since it is the default font in many word processing programs. Other acceptable fonts are Bookman, New Century Schoolbook and Palatino. While they are all serif fonts, they do have different characteristics. The best way to determine which one you think would look best for your book is to print a page in each of the fonts you are considering. Make sure the page is printed with the margins and headings you have chosen. This will give you a realistic idea of how it will look on a page in your book.

When you set your book up as an e-book, you will want to us a sans serif font. It is easier to read on a screen than a serif font. You can use the same font that you used to write both your website and blog if you have them. Arial is the most common in writing today, but any word processing program has a number of them to choose from. Tahoma or Verdana are good sans serif faces for e-books. Do not use an odd looking font like Airmole.

PRINTING PROCESS

Like many other products, a manuscript has to go through a process before it becomes a book. Traditionally, books are printed on good paper and covered, or *bound*, in one of several ways. Books come in many cut sizes and their pages can come in different weights of paper. They can be bound in cloth, paper, or even plastic. You should have made these design decisions by now or have a good idea what you want. If you have not, then the take time to complete this step of the publishing process before you approach a printer. Printing is the most expensive part of producing a book and you need to ensure you make good decisions about your printing. A bad decision can cost thousands of dollars and leave you with a book that is not easily marketed.

By now your manuscript should have been edited, revised, designed, and formatted. You should have a camera-ready copy or PDF file, and a digital copy of the cover. You are now finally ready to have your book printed. If you are one of those people who excels at multi-tasking, you would have been looking for a printer while you were having the book typeset. Just keep in mind that submitting your book to a printer is only possible if you have had enough typesetting done to be sure of your page count. Printers cannot give you an estimate if they do not know exactly how many pages it will be and what kind of cover it will have. They also need to know if there will be any illustrations or colour on the inside. And finally, they need to know how many colours your cover will be printed in. That is a lot of things for you to have sorted out before you even approach a printer. At the same time, you cannot finish filling out some legal forms because you need to know how much your book is going to cost. The total amount is necessary to determine how much you will charge for it. As you can see, several things are tied into each other. Without one, you cannot have the other. Take the time you need right now to make sure you have covered all the necessary steps to be ready for the printer. If you make a mistake now, you can fix it. If you discover a mistake after the books are printed, you are stuck with them.

PRINTERS AND ESTIMATES

Before you have your book printed, you will need to get printer's price quotes from at least three different printers. Even if you live in a small community with only one printing firm, get several quotes from nearby communities. If it becomes necessary to have your book printed out of town and your books shipped, do not hesitate to do so. Several books on self-publishing tell you to get quotes from as many as twenty-five printers. While it may be necessary in the United States, it is not necessary in Canada. We have far fewer printers here. Three or four at the very most, will be sufficient.

You want to have your books printed by

a *book printer*. A printing firm whose business is mostly made up of producing business cards and letterhead will not normally have either the knowledge nor the equipment to handle book print runs. Furthermore, if your first print run sells well, you need to be working with a printer who not only understands, but can handle, getting another one done in a timely fashion.

Appendix B shows a sample of what a printer's quote should look like. Make up the forms on your computer and print off as many as you need. Fill in the details as completely as possible about what you require. If a printer tells you all that information is not necessary, let them know that you really do require all that information. Do not be put off. If you get the sense a printer is not taking you seriously, take your business elsewhere. Remember you are a business person now. And right now your business is getting your book published.

In traditional offset printing, the more books you have printed the lower the cost. This is not as simple a statement as it seems. If you have used the formula to price your book accurately, you will know how much you can spend to have it printed and still make profit. A reasonable print run by a self-publisher in Canada is 500-1000 books, but 250-300 is quite acceptable too. A second print run does not cost nearly as much to produce since your book is already set up. Even though the estimate will indicate in hard numbers that larger printings are less costly, how much do you save if you end up with one or two or three or five thousand unsold books in your basement or garage? It is better to spend a few more pennies per book up front and not have to worry about storage - especially long term. Do not be miserly or you could end up regretting your decision to self-publish at all.

TYPES OF PRINTING

Today there is a wide variety of types of printers. You can have a large book run done at an offset printer or have your book printed one at a time by a print-on-demand (POD) printer. You can even have it photocopied on very sophisticated and expensive machines. Some use ink and some use laser. Others do not even use paper - your book is online. It can be very confusing for a first time publisher. You need to find the printer that best suits your needs and those of your book. While you should ask advice of others who have gone the self-publishing route, do not let their views sway you. After all, this is your book and you know best how to present it to the world. I know two people who have had books printed by a POD printer that I would not give a dime to. And yet they were happy with the result. At the same time, they would not go near an offset printer, which is what I use because I need larger print runs. Take your time at this step and do your homework. Printing is where most of your money goes and you do not want it wasted.

Offset printing

Most books have been published by offset printing since World War II. First, you must make sure your manuscript is *camera ready*. This is done at the time of typesetting. The copy must be on high-grade paper and can be either laser printed or printed with a good quality inkjet printer. For the latter, use a high dots-per-inch (dpi) and the darkest black ink. The best thing to do is to put a new ink cartridge in the printer to ensure the clearest colour. If you can afford it, purchase a good quality laser printer for this job. Print all of the pages at the same time so there is a consistency to the print. Otherwise you could end up with some pages having darker text than others.

The offset printer takes these pages, photographs them, and makes a negative of them. Thin plates are made and bent over cylinders or drums. The text and illustration images are then etched into the surface. The ink will adhere to the etched areas only. Next to this drum is another one that is covered with a rubber blanket onto which the plate *offsets* the images. The rubber covered drum rolls against the paper and prints on it.

Many books on self-publishing advise

you to have metal plates made and then keep them for reprints. Today most printers use disposable plates (called *silver*) that are meant to be used only one time. The cost should be no higher than for metal because this method is actually less expensive. Discuss this with your printer. If your chosen printer does use metal plates, make sure it is clear in your contract that the plates are your property.

More offset printers are investing in expensive equipment and can print from a digital file. This makes your job easier. You simply have to turn your typeset file into a PDF file and save it to a CD. You might even be able to e-mail it to your printer. Make sure you go through the whole PDF file before sending it along. You want to catch formatting mistakes before they show up in your book.

Offset printing is the way trade publishers make books. Some have their own press but more and more are contracting out to large professional firm that specialize in book printing. Some have whole departments to handle this fairly technical aspect of producing a book, but you have just yourself and the printer you decide to hire. Try and find a printer who specializes in books rather than flyers, business cards, and stationery. The latter may not be helpful to you because books are not their specialty. And do not be afraid to have your books printed in another city or even another province. If there is no one in your region who can do a professional job, you might have to go elsewhere. Often the cost of shipping is factored into the cost of the book. Never take a chance that your book will look amateurish. This will make it harder to sell.

Ask your printer questions about the process they use. Have them go over any part of the sequence that you do not understand. Do not be intimidated if they seem impatient. This is the largest outlay of money for a self-publisher and you have every right to know exactly how it is being spent. You should always have with you the Request For Quotation (RFQ) from the printer you chose so that you can refer to it often.

The primary advantage of offset printing is its ability to produce photographs and illustrations. You will also be able to have your book done in any trim size and bound as you wish. If you need a special size trim or want a hardcover, this is the best way to go. The disadvantage to this method of printing is that, the larger the print run, the lower the cost per book. Even if you decide to order a relatively small print run of 250 and pay the extra cost, you still have to have a minimum number of books printed. This forces you to find storage space for all those boxes of books. This drawback has led to the birth of a whole new type of printing process that seems geared for self-publishers.

Digital Printing

The print-on-demand (POD) or digital printer, differs from offset and can be useful for self-publishers. You do not have to order thousands or even hundreds of books and then have to find storage space. You can have as few as one book done at a time. The production cost is supposed to be the same for each book, although the reality is that the more books you order the better the price because of the cost of paper. This can make it easier for you to handle orders. All you need to do is order the number that you expect will sell in the near future rather than trying to guess what your whole future market might be. And most digital printers can provide a fairly quick turn-around time for reprints. It sounds like a perfect solution.

The digital method of printing actually uses a very high-end computerized copier type of machine. Besides the ability to print only the number of books you need, another advantage is that they are set up to have your typeset book put into the machine from either a CD or electronic file. This means you do not have to have a camera ready copy made. Instead you will make a PDF file. Although you should provide a hard copy for the printer to refer to, the machine can make your book straight from a disk or e-mailed file.

The main drawback to this type of

printing are the printers themselves. Anyone who can afford to lease one of these machines can call themselves a POD printer. The internet is full of websites touting their services. But do they really know anything about the publishing process? Like all other aspects of business, do your research. Make sure you get not only price quotes, but references from other clients who have had books published. Take a look at other books the printer has done. Do they meet your expectation of a professional looking product? Too many new self-publishers are paying out too much money for an inferior product. It is not that most POD printers are deliberately taking advantage, they often do not know better themselves.

Another drawback to using digital printers is the type of cover they can provide. Most of them cannot do hard covers while others limit the size of the book due to the inefficiency of their binding machines. Many successful book packagers limit the number of pages of your book because they can only produce a book up to a certain page size. This severely restricts their service to you. You then have to either change the size of your book, change the font and leading, or change the number of pages with a serious rewrite. If your book is fairly small, digital printing might be optimum. If you want it to have a hard cover or wish to keep the length, go to an offset printer.

Digital printers are good for small print runs and small books. They are also good for reprints of out-of-print books. They work well for family histories or books put together by an organization to raise money for its cause. They do fill a need in the self-publishing world. What you have to do is determine if they fill your need too.

E-books

You may decide to make your work available online as an e-book. This means you will not have to worry about printing or binding. There would be no paper to buy nor covers to have printed. Your book would be available as a *portable document format* (PDF) file to download from your website. It would be set up to be downloaded into the customer's computer after they have paid for it, normally via PayPal. You can also produce your book in the format of popular readers such as Sony Reader, Amazon Kindle, Indigo Kobo and Barnes&Noble's Nook. Books can also be read on smartphones like iPhone and BlackBerry, and tablets such as iPad and BlackBerry PlayBook. Adobe InDesign has a feature that allows you to convert to an EPUB format. Also there are websites such as **www.smashwords. com** that will convert your file into a format for readers. Do your research and find the best way for you to convert files.

Your manuscript must be on a disk or CD in order to make it available online. It must be formatted on the disk. If you decide to go this route, then you will need a PayPal account so people can pay. Do not take credit cards online. Another option is to place your book in several online bookstores made specifically for e-books. For a discount, they will collect payment for your book.

More and more you should have both e-books and print copies made to cover both virtual and real bookstores. You might want to consider this as part of your marketing plan. Start out by offering an e-book and, if the market interest is high, have print copies made. Or launch both simultaneously. Just make sure your marketing plan allows for this. Even though most readers still prefer to curl up with a good made-of-paper volume, the younger generation is embracing today's technology.

Another option is to make your book available as a CD. People who love books and stories often listen to CDs when they are on long trips or making the long commute to and from work. Audio books are becoming more popular for those who cannot make the time to read.

PROOF COPY

After your printer has set up the first

copy of your book into their software, you should receive a proof copy. What you are sent as a proof copy or blueline, will depend on what the printing company uses. Ask when you order your books. One offset company we dealt with sent out a proof copy actually on blue paper with specific instructions on how make corrections, including what colour of ink to use. A digital printer we have dealt with couriered a proof book complete with cover that we could mark up any way we chose. Proof copies are even emailed. No matter what you receive to proof, remember this is your last chance to make corrections. The next time you see your book, it will be one of how ever many hundred or thousand you chose to have printed. Remember that one mistake will be multiplied by that number.

I cannot emphasize the importance of going over the proof copy thoroughly. Although you should have caught all the spelling mistakes, I can almost guarantee you will find another one or two. But what you are looking for are the formatting mistakes that you missed in your excitement to send your PDF file to the printer. Too many self-publishers do not take the time to go through their PDF file slowly and carefully. It is not until the proof copy shows up that they see glaring formatting mistakes. Sometimes the font changes on some pages or the leading is tighter in some paragraphs. You need to go through the proof copy page by page. To have a good looking product, the interior components must be consistent. Some of the things you need to look for are:

- ✓ All the running heads are identically spaced from the top of the book
- ✓ All the text in the running heads is consistent throughout the book
- ✓ All the indents are the same number of spaces
- ✓ The first page of each chapter is consistent in terms of design
- ✓ Page numbers are in the same place on each page
- ✓ Page number font and size is consistent throughout the book
- ✓ Each component of the front matter and back matter is in the right order
- ✓ Ensure the page numbers in the table of contents are accurate
- ✓ Spacing between sections or paragraphs is consistent

BINDING

If you decide to print your book, it must be put together and covered. This is called *binding*. Books can be covered in paper, cloth, or leather. Paper is the most commonly used medium today because cloth and leather are fairly expensive. These latter two often come with a book jacket to protect them. Do not mistake a softcover book for a mass published paperback. The former is like the book you are reading and the latter is a pocket novel. Take a look at any of these you have around the house and you can see the difference in quality. Pocket novels are meant to be inexpensive because they are produced in large quantities.

The binding process involves putting together the galleys of your book. Depending on what printing company you have decided on, your pages could either be printed out in a stack or on large press sheets. With a stack, the book is bound and then cut to size. Larger sheets first have to be folded and collated, and then bound. They must be sized before binding. Many older books about self-publishing go into detail about this process. It is not necessary for you to be concerned about the *signatures* unless your offset printer brings to your attention that you have an odd number of pages. By this I mean that your book length is not divisible by 32, 16, or 8. In which case, you end up paying for unused pages. Digital printers do not use signatures.

A common question many first time self-publisher's have is whether to laminate their soft covers. The answer is an unequivocal "yes". Some digital printers will recommend against it since they claim humidity can make the covers curl. This tells you they are not using a very good quality laminating material.

Sometimes the oil in the digitally printed cover, especially a dark colour, will not adhere to the laminating. Again, this is not good quality laminating material.

Professional binders use a laminating material that does not curl and that will adhere to dark colours. What laminating does is protect the cover of your book. You cannot sell books that have acquired scuff marks from rubbing against other books in the box. Laminated covers will protect against scuffing and keep their appearance well. Often libraries and booksellers will not even look at a book that is not laminated.

AFTER PRESS

After your books are printed, you need to check them carefully. An average size printer paper box will hold 80-90 books. Open your boxes up and randomly select books. Look at the cover to make sure there is no damage or scuff marks. Set aside all damaged books and return them to the printer or binder. Take the rest home and get ready to set your marketing plan in motion.

Your books should be printed at least three months before your release date. Too often self-publishers get their books a week or two (or less) before the release date. Publishers do not work with such a short turn-around time because they know they need copies on hand to send out for reviews. Their distributors will need to have the books before the release date too. Pre-release copies also need to be sent to reviewers. You will learn more about how to get reviews in a later chapter. For now, enjoy the fact that you are an author. You have written and published a book - a feat which many dream of and few ever realize. Now the hard work begins.

CHAPTER FIVE

Minding Your Self-Publishing Business

The single most valuable skill in business ...
is the ability to make the right decisions
most of the time.
— Charles Templeton

HOME-BASED BUSINESS

For many of you, this will be the first time you have ever run your own business. While the business of self-publishing will probably not make you rich, it is still a business with all the ensuing decisions and problems that come along with it. You have to claim income, pay taxes, and keep books. You might make a profit and you might not. Few people are highly successful in self-publishing. Of course, you may not be in this for money at all. In order to at least recover your investment, you need to pay close attention to managing your self-publishing business.

Some of you will have already experienced the joys of self employment. You may have a wealth of knowledge about running a small or home-based business. You will also understand some of the pitfalls awaiting you. And you know from first-hand experience the thrill of making your own decisions, right or wrong. For those of you who have never tried self-employment, this chapter suggests some ideas to help you out. In addition, you can easily find business books in libraries, bookstores, and financial institutions. Federal and provincial governments, as well as banks, give them away for free. To be honest, it is possible to end up with a fairly large library of *how-to* and *where-to-find* books, so try not to go overboard.

NAME

Every business needs a distinctive name. The name should be unique and easy to remember. It may or may not describe the products and services you provide. In today's online market, it needs to work with a *dot-com* or *dot-ca* domain. If it is too long, it will be a problem for any perspective customer to type it correctly. You also want to make sure the name you choose is available in a domain.

Write out several names that you like.

Then go to the library and look up PUBLISHERS in *RR Bowker's Books in Print*. (Note: you cannot look them up online unless you are a paid subscriber). See if the name you want is already taken. Under certain circumstances, you may use an untrademarked business name that is being used by someone in another province or country, but that is not advisable. If the other business has a bad reputation, you will get to share that too. It is best to come up with an original name for your business.

Many self-publishing experts recommend that you not use your own name as in *John Doe Publishing*. If you do, it will be a dead giveaway that you are an author-publisher. Even though this might sound deceitful, it is done because you do not always benefit from being known as a self-publisher. At the same time, many large publishing companies are made up of the owner's surnames, such as McClelland & Stewart Inc., and it comes across as sophisticated. To be honest, along the way you cannot completely hide the fact you are an independent publisher. You may want to call your small publishing business by your own name to keep branding simple. Cute names can either well work for you or very much against you. Keep that in mind when you choose. And do not pick something offensive or you will find prospective customers turned off before they even look at your book. Give the business name a lot of thought. It is your choice how you wish to proceed.

At this stage you will probably have only one book on your list. Be aware that some distributors and bookstores will not even deal with a publisher who does not have a decent sized book list. But do not be deterred. At the very least, you will have local sales and personal tax deductions.

In some Canadian provinces and territories you do not have to register the name of your business if you actually do business under your own name such as *John Doe Publishing*. You are only required to register the name if you use a trade name (ie: *Half Acre Publishing*), or have another person or persons in the name as in *John Doe and Sons*. In other provinces and territories you are required to have all business names searched for a fee, and then register the business name for another fee. Fees vary across the country. To find out if you have to register a business name in your province or territory, visit the Canada Business website at **www.canadabusiness.ca** where you will find easy to understand and detailed information on starting a business in your province or territory.

Now you have to decide if you want your self-publishing business to be a *proprietorship* or a *partnership*. A proprietorship is a business that is owned and operated by one person. A partnership is a business that one or more other people also own and operate with you. Be very sure of the person or persons you are going into business with if you are forming a partnership. Both types of small businesses are tied into your personal income. Make sure all contracts are looked at by a lawyer. A third option is to *incorporate*. Unless your business grows substantially, it is not the best way to start out because it can cost a lot of money. The major advantage to incorporating is that the business is responsible for any debts incurred, rather than you personally. Unfortunately, at this time, many large companies want personal guarantees. A good accountant can give you sound advice on the tax strategies that will work best for you and your business. Information on incorporating in the provinces and territories is found at the Canada Business website.

BUSINESS NUMBER

In January 1995, Revenue Canada introduced a business identification system to simplify the process of starting a business. The Business Number (BN) system replaces all the numbers once required to conduct business in Canada. It includes the GST/HST, payroll deductions, corporate income tax, import/export accounts and other federal and provincial accounts. There is no fee at this time and you can register for a BN at **www. canadabusiness.ca**.

If you do not intend to collect GST/HST, will not have employees, are not incorporated, and do not plan to import or export products, then you do not require a BN. Please do not waste either your time or the governments by applying for one. If you do well and find your business needs a BN, you can apply at that time.

GST/HST

Since its inception, we have all learned to live with the Goods and Services Tax. Nova Scotia, New Brunswick, Newfoundland and Labrador, Ontario and British Columbia have implemented the HST or Harmonized Sales Tax which blends their GST and PST into one tax. And, to the deep sorrow of many, most books sold in Canada are taxable. No province at this time is charging Provincial Sales Tax on books, but they are subject to federal tax. All provinces who have HST also charge the whole amount on books.

If your business grosses more than $30,000 per year, you are required to collect GST/HST for the government. Then you have to remit their share. Probably the only reason you would get a Business Number would be to collect GST/HST. You collect 7% on each book, hang on to it until you get your statement, and then you send it in. It is pretty simple actually. If you live in an HST province, you are not required to collect more than the GST portion of 7%. If you are unsure how to proceed, obtain the GST/HST information guide from Business Canada online or ask your accountant.

You do not have to register for GST/HST if your business' gross taxable revenue is less than $30,000 per year. If you do not register, you can use all the GST/HST that you pay as an allowable expense rather than become a GST/HST collector. This can be a large tax advantage for you depending on your personal income. Speak to an accountant.

You are allowed to register even if your business is under $30,000 per year. There are two ways to proceed. If you do register, then everything you pay GST/HST on is refunded to you. For example, consider the cost of printing. For every $1000 you spend, you will pay $70 in GST or more in HST. Wouldn't it be nice to get that back? You will have paid for typesetting services, bought stationery supplies, paid for book production, and a myriad of other business necessities. You might as well get some of the money back directly. And if your book sells well, then you already have the account in place. You collect the GST/HST like you would for any business. The difference is when you make your remittance. If you paid out more GST/HST than you collected, the government lets you keep that and will even send you a cheque for the difference. It is important to discuss GST/HST options with your accountant.

When you register you will be asked if

you want to remit annually or quarterly. It is tempting to do the paperwork once a year only. But remitting quarterly has its advantages. First, if the government owes you money, you will receive it sooner. This can be very helpful in the early days of your business when you need to maximize cash flow. For example, if your book is released in the spring, you will not receive any money until the following year. Second, if you owe the government, you do not have to keep the money for very long. Surprisingly, this can be a problem for many entrepreneurs, and unpaid portions can result in legal action by the federal government. Do your bookkeeping carefully to make sure you do not spend the government's portion. It might be better to pay them quarterly and be done with it.

People are often intimidated by government paperwork. The GST/HST remittance form is very easy to complete. It is a fill-in-the-blanks form with instructions on each line. It is only a single page long with a working section at the top, and a detachable section you send in. All pertinent business information is preprinted on the form. They even include an envelope. Do not be afraid of GST/HST. It is simply a part of doing business.

BANK ACCOUNT

After you have a name and BN, you

need to open a business account at a financial institution. Each bank and credit union has its own procedures. Most, though, have a business department. Make an appointment to see someone to help you set up the kind of account you will need. Carefully explain the kind of business you will be running so you can get the best advice.

Some business bank representatives will give you booklets and information on being in business for yourself. Some might even want you to write a business plan. You have to decide what is right for your self-publishing business. If you are only going to have a short printing of a local history and never plan to write another book, you do not really need to write a business plan. On the other hand if you think you are going to self-publish books for many years, it is a good idea to put one together. Business plans are useful for successful business. Discuss this with your bank representative.

Your business account at a financial institution will need to be a chequing account. This is the best way to keep track of money deposited and spent. It will help your accountant figure out profits and losses at tax time. You should receive a statement once a month which allows you to reconcile the account. This is done just like you do with your personal chequing account, assuming you reconcile your personal account. Your financial institutions will give you a bank card that you can use to make deposits or withdrawals. The convenience of being able to make deposits anytime is very valid. I recommend, though, that you make it a practice to withdraw funds only by cheque. That is still the best way to keep a paper trail.

BOOKKEEPING

Some of you might enjoy the prospect of keeping a set of books. Others of you will have an anxiety attack. There seems to be no middle ground on the subject. But businesses must keep accurate records, and bookkeeping is one of the necessary evils that come with the deal. If the books are set up properly during the start up of a business, and kept up, they should not pose a problem. There is also the question of whether to do the books manually or on the computer. This is a personal decision. If you do not feel comfortable with a computer, you should do your record keeping manually. Launching a small business is not the time to learn how to use new software. When I published my first book, I did not think the sales volume on a single product justified using a computer bookkeeping program. I used a standard ledger and file folders for all my receipts. Now we keep our ledger in a spreadsheet program. Do whatever feels most comfortable for you.

If you have no experience with

bookkeeping, and maybe have problems keeping your personal accounts in order, you should probably find someone to help you. It is not necessary to hire a service (unless you want to). You can have a partner, family member, or friend help you set up and maintain the books. The important thing is to keep the books up to date. An accountant once told me if I brought my year end books into his office in a plastic garbage bag, he would charge me accordingly. In other words, the cost of having an accounting firm clean up your bookkeeping mess is pretty high. A little housekeeping on your part will keep that from happening to you.

Putting your books together and taking them to an accountant is important for filing your income taxes. Accountants know how the tax system works and keep up to date on tax regulations. There is a fee for having an accountant do your year end paperwork, but it is tax deductible. Consider that you will probably receive a larger refund by having a professional take care of the year end stuff and you will see it is worth the cost. Whether you use the services of a Chartered Accountant or a Certified General Accountant is strictly up to you. Many CGA specialize in small business. Find accountants in your phone book and ask others business people who they use. Recommendations are the most valuable way to find a good accountant.

CREDIT CARDS

When you are in a business that sells a retail product, some customers will want to make purchases with their credit card. Depending on how you market your book, you may or may not want to offer that service. The first thing to know is that it costs money to offer sales by credit card. Service fees can get rather high. The second, and very important, thing to know is that you have a liability for taking a stolen card. This alone puts many small businesses off from being a merchant. If you do decide to take credit cards, make sure you take both Visa and Mastercard. And make sure you read your contract so you have no surprises.

All online sales should be paid via a service such as PayPal. If you take credit cards directly through your website, you may find yourself responsible for all costs for a stolen card. Do not do it. Online payment services are easy to set up and the fees are low. Someone else has the responsibility and you will be notified by email when a payment for product comes in.

You do not need to offer credit card sales if you expect to market your books through a distributor or wholesaler, since you will not be selling directly to the consumer. If you even sell just to local bookstores you will not need that either because bookstores should be invoiced by you. It is when you sell directly to customers that they will ask if they can pay with a card. I recommend you talk this over with your accountant and bank representative before making the decision. Fortunately, it is not one you have to make when you are just starting out.

PAYPAL

PayPal is an e-commerce business that allows payments and money transfers to be made through the internet. It is an account based system that lets anyone with an email address securely send and receive online payments using their credit card or bank account. It is the most popular way to electronically pay for product purchased online and it is an inexpensive way for merchants to accept credit cards. You can use it to both collect payment from customers and to email invoices for online payment.

PayPal is easy to set up and the site provides the buttons you will need for your website. It works with most major shopping carts. The fees are reasonable and the fee structure is the same for both personal and business accounts. When you want the money, you simply transfer it to your bank account.

PayPal is a great way to get paid quickly. When you log on, you will be able to view business reports and logs. And one of the best things about using PayPal is that the seller is protected from fraud.

Managing your self-publishing business will be an adventure. It can either be an exciting adventure or a frustrating one, depending on how well you keep on top of the business details. If you are unsure of this part of self-publishing, get someone to help you. Do not let the task of bookkeeping take away the joy of producing a book in print. Remember that you will be wearing many hats. And one of them has to be the businessperson's hat.

CHAPTER SIX

Before the Release Date

Doing business without advertising is like winking at a pretty girl in the dark - you know what you're doing, but nobody else does.

— Murray Koffler

PRE-PUBLICATION

A book is not considered to be actually published until it is finally released for the public to purchase and read. Until then, you have even more work to do in order to give your book the best chance in the marketplace. By now, you should have started your own publishing business, and have a completely formatted book, which should be either at the printer or ready to go. You should have decided on cost, page count, and the date of publication (or release). If you have planned properly, you will be well within your schedule. Now the real work begins.

In the trade publishing industry, books can take as much as a year or two from the time the manuscript is accepted until it is made available to the public in bookstores and libraries. During the process of making a book, the editor is busy preparing the press and bookstores for release of the book. Giving out this information usually takes place about six months before the release date. I do not recommend you put it off for any less than three or four months, or you may not be viewed kindly by either reviewers or distributors. One of the main reasons these people do not like to accept self-published material is because it is not usually offered in either a professional manner or time frame. Pre-publicity must be factored into your schedule.

Pre-publication is a very important step to self publishing. If you do it well, it may be what sells your book. If you do it badly, you may end up regretting that you ever tried to publish a book yourself. If you are shy about "tooting your own horn" you might need help at this step. Publicists and publicity firms come in all price ranges. On the other hand, your skills as a writer will serve you well at this stage. You can send out packages to reviewers, register with all the industry databases, and write news releases and advertisements. Your business self and your writing self blend at this point.

MARKETING PLAN

Most endeavours in this world are more successful when there is a plan in place. You need a marketing plan in order to have a step-by-step "map" to guide you through the process of selling your book. The easiest way to start is by brainstorming ideas and writing them down. Get friends and family involved in this kind of session. After you complete the list, you can start to look at what you are prepared to do to sell books.

Begin by deciding the level of marketing you plan to do - national, regional, or local. Make a list of the print media and broadcast media you want to send press packages to. Put together a list of people who you would like testimonials from. Then write a letter of request for testimonials from each one of them. The next list to make is that of any newsletters, printed or online, that you think might be interested in your book. These tend to be topical and have a dedicated readership. Then list the booksellers you plan to approach, along with their contact information. What a lot of lists to make! And you could use more - lists of where you want to have book signings, lists of catalogues that might carry your book, lists of media where you might want to place paid ads, and on and on. Be creative and you might surprise yourself at how many venues you come up with to publicize your book. The next chapter covers marketing in more detail and you may want to add those ideas to the lists that you have made.

Part of your marketing plan should include writing a first draft of your news release and any articles you think might appeal to print media on your lists. You can write final drafts later. If you can come up with more than one angle for your material, write more than one article. Make a list of website designers or research web templates. Decide what you want to put on your website. Make a list of keywords and reciprocal links for your website, and set up a press room on your website.

As you can see, devising a marketing plan requires a lot of creative thinking. Actually, it is mostly thinking and writing down ideas. From these, you will "fill in the blanks" with names and contact information. Each time you read about something or come up with another idea, write it down. I keep a file folder handy to put all the lists and notes into as they accumulate. I label it "Marketing" and that way I will not lose any ideas or information that I have collected. Your marketing plan and file containing information will help you to stay organized. When things start to take off, you will appreciate feeling like you are organized somewhere.

LISTS AND DATABASES

Before your book goes to print, you will

need to order the CIP information to put on the legal page. This was discussed in Chapter 3. By taking part in the CIP program, your book will automatically be put into their catalogue and database. Also make time to pull together the information and fill out the *New Book Service.* This will increase your exposure.

Another important database I have already discussed is R.R. Bowker's *Books in Print* and *Global Books in Print.* This is a huge database that will put your book into their electronic catalogue. They offer information about millions of books to libraries and bookstores. They are obviously interested in listing self-published books, as there is an article on the subject on their website. There is no charge for any of these databases.

REVIEWS

Most of us have read book reviews in various newspapers. Many of the large dailies will do reviews, but smaller community papers also write them and it can result in a full page article with photos. Community papers will tie their story to you as a local author. Regional papers might also be willing to give you coverage because you are a provincial or regional author.

Reviews can be beneficial for your book sales. I cannot overemphasize their importance. In fact, the best thing you can do for your book is to get great reviews. As a self-publisher, the luckiest thing you can do is get any reviews. You may be told that reviewers will not look at self-published books. Truthfully, this is often the case. You are competing with established publishers who know most of the reviewers and produce a good product. It is not easy to have your book reviewed, so you have to carefully target the publications you want to send a review package out to.

Most reviews come from newspapers or a magazines. If you get a good review, you can have it printed on your book cover. You can excerpt a review and use only the part you need. Remember, though, to keep the spirit of what the reviewer had written or you will risk losing your credibility. You will need to make copies of all reviews and articles to include in your media package. Every time you receive a review, update your media package.

The most obvious place to start is Canada's large national papers, such as *The Globe and Mail* and *National Post*. If you think you have a book with national appeal, and can pitch it well, then send a book, or galley, and media package to the book review editor. You can find this information on their websites. Most of us do not have books with national appeal and we need to look closer to home for our reviews. The next place to look is your large regional or provincial daily newspaper. They might decide to review your book because you are a local author. Use this hook when you are preparing your media list. If they decide to profile you or your book, you might have to travel to the city where the newspaper is produced for a photo. If that is not possible, ensure you include a photo of yourself holding your book in your media package. We will discuss in detail what to put into a media package later in this chapter.

Many Canadian communities have small community newspapers that get delivered for no charge because the advertising covers the costs. Here is probably one of your best opportunities to get a review. Often you can get a half or full page write up along with a photo. You would be amazed at how widely newspapers of this type are distributed. If they had a subscription list, it would be quite large. Some of the community newspaper chains share stories and that will give a wider readership.

Magazines do not necessarily review books *per se*, but they do write articles about books. Authors often include their opinions about the material at the same time. A public library is the best place to find magazines that you would like to send your book, or galley, and media package to. You can look at current and back issues to determine if your subject matter is appropriate to that publication. Another place to look is *The Canadian Writer's Market*, which you should be able to find in any bookstore. Canadian magazines are listed, along with information on the kind of material they publish. If you can imagine your book's subject in there, put them on your list. If you think your book has a larger appeal, have a look at *Writer's Digest Writer's Market* to find American and international magazines you can contact. Always think about who would be interested in the subject of your book and how an article about your book might be received. Be prepared to write your own article, if necessary, to get the publicity.

Another source of reviews could be a person, sometimes an expert in the field or someone who is well known or whose opinion others respect. Start by looking for someone that you know, and who would be willing to read the manuscript or galley and give you their opinion. If they like the book and you like their opinion, ask them to write a review. Do not be surprised if you are expected to write it or pay a fee, though. Experts and well known people are asked so frequently to do things like this, they simply do not have time to write every testimonial or foreword that they are asked for.

Does paying negate the review? The answer is no. Reviewers for newspapers and writers for magazines are paid for what they do. As long as you are clear up front that the reviewer can say what they believe, do not worry about paying them. This is not the same as offering to pay someone to write a great review. Experts and well known people care about their reputation and can usually be counted on to give you an honest appraisal. And if you do not like the review, you do not have to use it.

A surprising part of the book publishing process is that you often have to write the review yourself. Again, well known people are usually very busy. What they want from you is a review that they can edit. It sounds odd, but that is often the way personal reviews are done. Writing your own review will be one of the hardest things for you to do. You have to say something dynamic about your book and try to keep in mind what your intended reviewer might say. Thinking in the third person takes some practice. While you might actually feel comfortable writing in the third person, it will seem strange to be writing about yourself and your book.

INFORMATION SHEETS

Just about everything you send out must include an information sheet about your book. Whether you submit material to the media or a catalogue, you need to provide certain information about your book. An information sheet should include the following:

- Book title
- Sub-title (if there is one)
- Author name
- Publication date
- ISBN
- Category or subject
- Number of pages and trim size
- Number of illustrations
- Price
- Publisher name and contact information
- Distributor contact (if being carried by one)

Some information sheets will require a short write up, or blurb, about the book. I recommend you write three of them - 30 words, 50 words, and 85 words. Keep them all handy because you will find that you are often required to tell about your book in a few words. For this book I built my blurbs one on the other. They all have the same beginning sentences, and I kept adding to each blurb until I got to my word count. It is also a great writing exercise for your writer self.

Many sources for information sheets tell you to include the name and contact information for the publicist. In this case that person is you! If you want to put on that hat on, so to speak, go ahead. Just remember, your name is the same as the author's.

INFORMATION SHEET

Title: Self Publishing in Canada
Subtitle: A complete guide to designing,   printing and selling your book

Author: Suzanne Anderson
Foreword by Dan Poynter
Category: Reference/Writing
ISBN; 978-1-894208-00-0
Non-Fiction
Softcover / 5.5" x 8.5" /288 pages
$24.95 (Cdn) plus shipping
Returns must be made within one year in new condition, prepackaged and prepaid.

Half Acre Publishing
3321 Renita Ridge Road
Duncan BC V9L 5J6
PH/FAX: 250-746-3919
halfacre@selfpublishing.ca
www.selfpublishing.ca

"Canada needs a book like this." Dan Poynter,   author of The Self-Publishing Manual

---

Figure 1

Of course this gives away the fact that the book is self-published. At the same time, if you act professionally and do not look silly, you will have a better chance of being noticed.

MEDIA PACKAGES

When you approach the media, whether it be print, radio or television, you need to provide a media package (press kit) in a presentation folder with your business card attached securely either on the inside or outside. If you choose to place your business card in the spot inside where the folder is cut for them, also make a label for the outside of the cover. Members of the media can get swamped with these packages. Sometimes they resemble business folders with other material in them and you want to make sure there is no doubt what is inside your folder. Everyone's desk gets covered at some time or another. Take the effort to ensure your press release does not get lost in the mess.

What goes into your media package? Every book you read on the subject and every website you visit will have different information. It can be confusing to a novice. Following is a list that will satisfy the needs of any member of the media and will show that you know what you are doing:

- An information sheet. If you had covers

printed on plain paper, you can print the information on the reverse side of them. This is a great idea if you are not sending a book or galley at this time.

- A letter clearly explaining why your book subject is important enough to be reviewed. Use a clear and active voice. This is your *pitch letter*, similar to that of a freelance writer trying to pitch an article to a magazine. Spend a lot of time writing it since it could be your only foot in the door.

- A news release, which I will describe later in this chapter.

- Author bio and photo. This is an opportunity to give details about yourself and establish both why you were the best person to write this book and what credentials you have. The photo should be no smaller than 5" x 7" and it does not matter if it is colour or black and white. Try to have a picture taken of you holding your book. If you have a digital camera and a computer, you can print your own public relations photos.

- A bookmark. Your cover designer can design one for you but you have to write the copy for it. They are a great marketing medium because people hang on to them. And booksellers love them.

- A page of testimonials if you have some by now. This shows a reviewer that others have read and appreciated your book. Make sure you write the quotes in italics and the name in regular font. If you are not submitting your information sheet on the extra covers of your book, print the testimonials on them instead. This will attract attention to your book.

Any time you receive a review, photocopy it and include it in all your media packages. Shrink a long review down to fit on either letter or legal size paper. Staple copies together if the review is on more than one page. Oddly enough, reviewers are more interested if others have reviewed your book. It tells them that your subject must be timely and interesting. It also tells them that someone else has considered your book seriously enough to write about it.

Offer to write an article for other publications if you have that skill. Many times that will be the only way to get publicity for your book. Small print media and busy ones both will look favourably at an offer of an article. It is important, though, that you know how to write in this specialized format. It is very different from writing a book. Word count is important and, like a news release, it has a standard format. While an article is not as structured as a news release, the standard format still has to be followed. Most local colleges offer courses or workshops on article or freelance writing. It might be a worthwhile investment for you to take one.

NEWS RELEASE

A news release, or press release, is a great way to publicize your book. Small newspapers will often run it as is. Larger newspapers might run it as you have written it or use parts of it as filler. Either way, it is free. If you do not know how to write a news release, check on the internet or for books on the subject that even have samples in them. If you really cannot write a news release, find someone else to do it for you. This is one time it is worthwhile to pay someone to write for you.

Your release should be on 8" x 11" paper and kept to one page in length. Your headline needs to grab the reader's attention. Figure out a "hook" and keep to that theme. Remember to use the five "W's" in your first paragraph - *who, what, where, when, why*, and sometimes *how*. Each succeeding paragraph should be of declining importance in case the press release needs to be shortened. You do not want to have important information chopped off. Use short words and sentences. This is for a newspaper and they have a specific way they want copy written. If you are still in doubt, have a good look at some newspapers. Check out newspapers in your nearest big city, your own town, and nationally. The illustration on page 147 is a sample of a news release.

How do you get a news release out to the media? If it is not in a press package, either email or FAX it. Although the technology is in place, many media outlets still do not take press releases by email. Even the smallest of papers often receive news releases and CP information via their FAX machine. If the media you are sending your news release to prefers emailed submissions, do not send the press release as an attachment. Most media do not open attachments because they could contain a virus. Copy and paste the release into the body of the email. Make a concise signature block in your email program and use it every time you send anything. Include your name, contact information, web address and the name of your book.

ADVERTISING

Surprisingly, many people are not quite sure what the difference is between *publicity* and *advertising*. Publicity usually comes free of charge and advertising normally requires payment. Publicity is a news release or article in the local paper, while advertising is a paid advertisement in the same paper. You want

FOR IMMEDIATE RELEASE

Contact: Suzanne Anderson
          Half Acre Publishing
          3321 Renita Ridge Road
          Duncan BC V9L 5J6
          Phone/FAX: 250-746-3919
          info@selfpublishing.ca
          www.selfpublishing.ca

SELF-PUBLISHING IN CANADA NOW EASIER

(Duncan, BC, January 3, 2004) –As self-publishing fast becomes a real option in Canada, a source of current information for both the beginner and the more experienced author has appeared on the horizon. Half Acre Publishing announced today the publication of a new book entitled SELF PUBLISHING IN CANADA – A COMPLETE GUIDE TO DESIGNING, PRINTING AND SELLING YOUR BOOK by Suzanne Anderson. Delivering accurate book design standards and current internet resources, this book will help the self-publisher compete for shelf space in bookstores.

Self-publishing is no longer the last resort of a desperate writer. Given today's technology, it is a valid option that is rapidly gaining popularity in Canada. With the demise of General Distribution Services, and the ensuing fallout, more and more writers are turning to the independent method of publishing in order to get their books in the hands of the reading public. Now there is a book available that will unlock the secrets to self-publishing in Canada.

Anderson is an experienced self-published author. She has worked as a freelance writer and is currently on the board of directors for a self-publishing co-operative on Vancouver Island. She conducts workshops on self-publishing at various colleges and universities. Visit her website at www.selfpublishing.ca

-30-

Figure 2

to try to gather as much publicity as possible, but sometimes it is worthwhile to pay for an ad.

When you decide to advertise, you really have to put on a business hat. The cost of ads can be very high and you want to spend no more than 5% of your total marketing budget on paid ads. You need to be creative to make the most of your advertising budget. A catch phrase today is to "think outside the box". Either devise an ad that gets your message across effectively or target specific media where you will be placing the ad. We all know the world of advertising is complex and we are mostly amateurs. So how do you know where to spend your money?

Canada's largest circulation newspaper about books is *BC Bookworld*. This western Canadian quarterly has more than 100,000 readers who include members of the industry and the general reading public. While anyone can subscribe and have it delivered, issues are free in many bookstores.

Catalogues are another good place to advertise. It can be reasonable to buy space in a book catalogue. Find out where the catalogue is being distributed and how many will be printed. Do not be surprised at the variance either. Catalogues run from 500 copies to 500,000. You will have to provide a list of information similar to the information sheet I have already discussed. You will also need to have a digital picture of the cover of your book. Actually, this is a good thing to have saved on a disk because you never know when the need will pop up. Make sure it is no larger than 100 dpi and saved in a JPG format. While some catalogues will take GIF or TIF files, pretty well everyone wants a JPG. More and more there are online book catalogues. Do not miss out on them either.

Radio is a medium that new author-publishers seldom think of. If your book has a wide audience you might consider Radio-TV Interview Report at **www.rtir.com**, which is a U.S. based directory of new books and is delivered to American TV and radio producers every couple of weeks.

Marketing professionals say the best place to spend your advertising dollar is by advertising not directly to the consumer, but in trade magazines that are read by librarians and booksellers. Their opinions are respected and, best of all, they make recommendations to their customers. In Canada we have *Quill & Quire* at **www.quillandquire.com** and *Canadian Bookseller* at **www.cbabook.org**.

However, there is no guarantee you will increase book sales by advertising. You could spend good money and not receive a single extra order for your efforts. That is why you need to put your business hat firmly on your head and make some serious decisions. Well placed and well planned ads can increase your chances of increasing book sales. But you may decide there is no need to advertise. Remember, most books still sell best by word-of-mouth. All the advertising dollars in the world cannot change that single fact. It is your call.

All this work needs to be done before you actually release your book. That means you have a lot of pre-planning to do. This aspect of self-publishing is very much on the business side. Those who love to write and hate to do business often do not like this aspect of self-publishing. Others find it challenging to come up with creative ways to sell books. Even if you do not like to do your own marketing, remember that books do not sell themselves and you really have to plan for getting your book out. If it is too uncomfortable for you, get help from a spouse, friend, or even a professional. Do not neglect this aspect of self-publishing. It is far too important.

CHAPTER SEVEN

Books for Sale!

*Radio is a 'hot' medium and is
indispensable when the issues get hot.
TV is a fantasy medium, and has good
reason to be called 'cool'.*
— Marshall McLuhan

MARKETING

Marketing is the most important step in the publishing process. Simply put, if you do not market your books they will not sell. In fact, they will end up sitting in boxes in your garage or basement taking up floor space. This crucial step is very definitely part of the business of self-publishing. You have to start to think of your books as products now - and products to be moved out quickly. This phase of self-publishing is where the real work begins.

There are almost as many ways to sell

books as there are books to be sold. You should already have your marketing plan made and be ready to activate it. This is the time to go over the plan to select which ideas you like from those you do not. Decide which ideas you think are feasible and decide which ones will work for your book. Now, finalize your list and start telling the world that you have books for sale.

WORD OF MOUTH

Believe it or not, the best marketing tool is word of mouth. When people read a book and like it, they tell their friends, who also read it and tell their friends. Many bestsellers have emerged as a result of this simple principle. One example is *The Christmas Box* by Richard Paul Evans. He wrote the story in 1994 for his daughters and printed a few copies for them and their friends. Every week he received requests for more books. He did not advertise, but every week he was printing more and more books. Finally, a large publisher made him a nice offer to publish the book. It has sold millions of copies around the world, proving how powerful word of mouth can be.

DIRECT MAIL

A popular way for an author-publisher to sell product is by direct mail where readers order books from your website and you mail the books out. This is a simple way to sell books. You do not have to deal with anyone in the middle such as a distributor or bookstore. If you are uncomfortable selling in person, this may be the best route for you. You gather orders that come through your website or by mail, and send out books. Just make sure you factor the cost of postage and envelopes into the total cost. These are business expenses and can be tax deductible. One advantage to selling this way is that you can charge less for the book since you will not have to look at discounts. Your books will sell for the price you set.

Certain types of books lend themselves more readily to mail order, usually non-fiction and how-to books. If you have done your research, you will have a clear idea of whether your book is right for mail order. If your market is made of people who would normally order by mail, you may do quite well. There are many good books about how to be successful with mail order sales. Invest in a few and educate yourself. People with a good product to sell have become financially successful this way.

The best place to advertise your mail order book for sale is on a website. You can also advertise in the classified sections of newspapers and magazines. Large newspapers will be more expensive than local ones, so decide where to find your market. Many specialty magazines have a classified section in the back. Surprisingly these can be a significant place to gather orders.

Write a small intriguing ad. Keep it brief because you pay by the word. You should not run the ad less than three issues since that is how long it normally takes to impress people. To "key" ads, make minor changes to your address such as adding a letter after the house number in the address. What this does is give you a clear picture where your books are selling. It can also be used to test various ads to see which draw the best response. Based on what you learn from keying your ad, make changes.

One proven method of successful mail order is to send order forms out to prospective customers. I do not recommend you use the addresses of everyone you have ever been associated with or are related to. Rather, purchase a mailing list to target your audience. They are not very expensive and are readily available on the internet. Decide who your potential readers are by either interest or demography, and contact a company that sells lists. You can either receive pre-printed labels or a computer file set up so you print the labels yourself. Check with the company you choose to see what their accuracy rate is. You do not want to spend money on a mail out campaign, only to have a large portion returned because the addresses are out of date. Treat it as a business transaction and you could be very successful. Like all other aspects of business, not doing your homework could add unnecessary costs.

Should you send out emails instead? At this time, I would not suggest it. People have strong spam filters and your ads could go directly into their trash file. Or you could end up being blocked. In order to be successful, you need to know about e-business and most self-publishers do not. If you think you would like to go in this direction, again educate yourself. There are a lot of websites and books about e-business.

ADVERTISEMENTS

To give your book publicity, you could take out paid advertisements in various newspapers and magazines. These are costly and need to be planned well in advance since your ad will compete with those of the trade publishers who are very proficient advertisers. Most self-publishers do not have the skills to even develop good ads. While the sales person at the publication can help with this, it still needs input from you. Advertising is a profession, and if you are not a professional, you are taking a chance with your investment money. The cost normally runs into the thousands of dollars, so you have to sell a lot of books to make it pay for itself. Many self-publishers believe in generating publicity, which is free, rather than paid advertising. There is merit to that belief.

There is a group of self-publishers who make a living advertising in the classified sections of magazines. They often have booklets for sale rather than books. Since this is a mail order method, the smaller product keeps the cost of postage down. Some people have been in business for decades selling books and booklets, and have become recognized as experts about their topic. Anything as simple as investment advice to recipes for zucchini will sell. You can often find courses online on how to sell this way. It might be worth checking out.

WEBSITES

We are in the information age and websites are as common as books. The internet is a great medium to sell just about anything, including books. It is an easy and inexpensive way to both promote and sell your book. Even if you are not comfortable with a computer, you need to give serious consideration to having your own website. A good site can promote your book, showcase you as an expert, and provide the media with material that you will not have to pay to mail. Your own website lets others know you are abreast of modern marketing techniques.

One big advantage to having your own

website is that you can sell e-books. You will need to have your book converted to several formats in order for people to be able to download them. I have already discussed how to make your book into readable files. Because you do not have many costs involved with this format, you can charge much less for the book. Although there are far more readers of paper books than e-books, the latter are becoming more and more popular.

There are sites on the internet that offer websites to authors, or you can set up your own. The cheapest method to set up your own site is to use the service your internet provider makes available. Most providers give you web space as part of your e-mail plan and usually run from two to five megabytes. You can easily sell one book in this amount of space. The web address would be *YourProvider.com/ YourSiteName/AnExtension.html*. This can be a bit long so make sure you use a short, catchy site name. But there is an alternative - you can have your own domain.

My domain is **www.selfpublishing.ca**. I could not get a .com or even a .net, but the .ca domains had just come out when I decided to purchase my own domain. More .ca domains are available than the older domain types. You can order a domain online from a firm such as **GoDaddy.com** or **Reg.ca**. GoDaddy has templates for making websites and will even host your site for a modest annual fee. The

Canadian Internet Registration Authority is responsible for registration and monitoring the .ca domains and can be found at **www.cira. ca.** You will pay a fee for registering as well as a small annual fee when you renew. Because the cost is reasonable, purchase a domain for you name too. Do not grab a bunch of domains that you do not need and sit on them. This is called "squatting" and is frowned upon. On the other hand, grab a domain if it will tie into a future project. That is considered good business sense.

Should you build your own site or have someone else do it? The answer depends a lot on your skills and abilities. If you have to get your nephew or the neighbour's kid to print your work out, then do not even attempt building a website. There are many arguments as to whether you should have a website built professionally or do it yourself. Everyone I talk to tells me it is easy. If you do it yourself you can either learn *html* (hyper text markup language) or you can use software that does it for you. This sounds easy, but really does you little good if you have no concept of good web design. Even a simple one page website requires some sense of design. As a writer you should appreciate that not anyone who can us a computer can write a book. Look at many sites before you decide if you can do it yourself. Some sites will even offer a template for a website and that might be a benefit for you.

If you decide to have someone else build your website, you need to decide who should do it. All of us have family members (usually high school or college students) who may offer to build your site. This is fine if you trust them. Make sure they show you their previous work. Then you need to show them sites you like and let them know what it is that you like about the sites. It may take a fairly long time to have a site built this way since most people really do not comprehend how complex it is to build even a simple site. Sometimes family members or friends cannot seem to grasp your vision. It can lead to frustration or even hard feelings. Like the editing process, do not risk relationships over business issues.

If you decide to either build the site yourself or have a friend or family member do it, you will have to find someone to host your site. You will be charged a set up fee and an annual fee. Unless you are a computer "guru" yourself, you will not understand how to get your site picked up by major search engines. It is no longer a matter of simply having the best *meta tags*. Today's web designer needs to understand search engine optimization (SEO). Research the internet for articles about SEO. Like any marketing medium, you need to ask your business self what you want from a website. If you want a simple, inexpensive site to promote your book, then look at doing it yourself. But when should you hire a professional? You should hire a professional when you need one.

I had family members attempt to build a site for me and it was not working out. I hired a professional web designer. I thought the cost was reasonable since I already knew what I wanted and was going to write all the text myself. The site was up in nine days and exceeded my expectations. All the hosting and editing is done by the webmaster and I can concentrate on what I know best - writing.

Now let us talk about the cost. Many of us go to family members or friends because we think it will cost $5,000 or more to have a site built. It can, but it should not be that much. Shop around and get estimates. Look at sites that the company has built and decide if you like their work. One local company I looked at had too many similarities among the sites they had built and I did not like that. Hosting can cost anywhere from $150 per year and up. Several technical questions need to be answered before you put your site up. A good designer not only knows the questions to ask, but they understand the answers.

Once the site is up, make sure all your pages load quickly or people will not stop to look at your site. Do not have too many graphics, banners or flashing icons because they are distracting. Your goal is to have a reader stop at your site and view your material. You might offer book excerpts or whole chapters. In fiction, post the first chapter and let viewers know they can read the rest of the book by ordering it. For non-fiction, consider posting the table of contents or the first page of each chapter. Synopsize some of the content and make a free report available. Make it easy for customers to order by setting up an account with PayPal or linking to an online bookstore such as Amazon.com where the book can be purchased directly. Make sure you can be contacted by both prospective readers and the media. Consider a "press room" at your site with a picture of yourself, a picture of the book, an author bio, news releases, story angles, and backgrounders. Also ensure that you provide links to other online sources. But do not just stop there, send a polite email to the webmaster of sites you would like to link to yours. This is called *reciprocal business* and can bring a lot of viewers to your site. Like all other marketing venues, a website should work for you and be within the budget you have planned. It is a business tool so do not let it take over your life.

SOCIAL NETWORKING

Self-publishers can benefit from online social networking sites to market books. Twitter, Facebook and blogs are very popular and warrant being considered as part of any marketing plan. I have used all three and find my personal favourite is Facebook. But that is my choice. I learned I cannot keep all three going at the same time and felt that Facebook best met my needs. You have to choose what works best for you.

Twitter is found at **www.twitter.com** and is intended for you to put out one or two lines of information known as microblogging. Twittering is simply short clips that convey the message. You acquire followers and you in turn follow others. If you choose this medium, be careful who you follow. Make sure they are relevant to your topic. Twitter requires constant input. You might want to write up several short messages before you even sign up. Then you can just put them up on a regular schedule.

Facebook is huge and growing daily. Many of you might even have a personal Facebook page. What you want to set up is a Facebook Business Page. It allows you to advertise your business and products within the Facebook user community. And it is very easy to set up. Go to **http://www.facebook.com/pages/create.php** and follow the prompts. I recommend you set up a separate business email address so you are not using your personal one. Many providers these days will allow you to set up several email addresses for yourself, so use that feature. If your provider does not have that feature, then set up an account with Hotmail, Yahoo or Gmail. On Facebook there is a box to upload a logo photo but the best image for you to put into that box is a JPG of the cover of your book. Add content and links to articles and related sites at least once a week. Facebook will send updates of how many people visit your site and other data to help you track your market.

A blog is a web log or web journal. They are posted online for a number of topics, whether fiction or non-fiction. Some authors share their writing in their blog. Some trade publishers look for potential clients by checking out writer's blogs. If you have written about a pertinent topic, you can also blog about it. You can encourage readers to buy your book or you can comment on aspects of your subject or even use it to update material about your subject. A blog can be short or long, but it has to be interesting. It can take up a lot of your time to keep a blog current. You should post once a week or more often.

There are other social networking sites too, such as MySpace and LinkedIn. The latter is for business and professional networking. Check them all out. But do not get so wrapped up in social networking that you neglect your marketing plan. As nice as social networking is, it is not necessarily the best way to sell books. You need to read your book, talk about your book, and get it into the hands of readers. Use social networking as a part of your marketing plan, but not the whole basis for it.

BOOKSTORES - REAL AND ONLINE

The obvious place to take your books to sell are bookstores. Unfortunately it is not as easy to place your books in them as it once was. Not too many years ago, an independent bookstore would take a few books if you presented yourself professionally. The managers of large chains had small budgets for local books and would talk to you about carrying your book. If you presented terms that were within industry standards, including a return policy, you stood a fair chance of getting your book on a shelf somewhere. Now you pretty much have to either have a distributor or offer the book on consignment. It is time consuming and expensive for a bookstore to set up an account for your little publishing company that has only one book. Actually, many experienced author-publishers will tell you bookstores are the worst places to try to sell books. Consumers purchase more books in specialty stores these days.

You can still try to have a bookstore purchase your book if you feel it is important though. Your presentation has to be professional and meet industry standards. Bookstores receive a minimum 40% discount, Chapters Indigo receives 45% and there is no negotiating. Many distributors offer a sliding scale to encourage more sales. Your return policy must be stated clearly. The norm is that you will take the books back in good condition, prepackaged and prepaid, within a year from purchase. The sad reality is that most books are not in good condition when you get them back. You will also find that the definition of good condition is open to interpretation. You are not required to refund the bookstore for books that look like they have been well used. When you sell to bookstores, you have to make sure you have the funds held back to pay them for returns that are in good condition.

Online bookstores do not normally buy books, so you do not have to deal with the hassle of returns. They usually require a setup fee and a percentage of the price of any of your books they sell. They will place your book on their website and customers purchase from them, so you do not have to worry about handling online orders. **Amazon.com** is the largest and most recognized online bookstore in the world, but there are many other smaller ones. Run a Google search and you will find many online bookstores to choose from. Some online bookstores will warehouse a few copies, but do not expect that. Keep your reputation intact by ensuring that you send the books out within two to four days after you receive the order. Research the various sites and requirements carefully. For online bookstores, make sure you have a good quality JPG digital photo of your book's front cover ready to send to them, along with a short catchy blurb. This is all the reader will see, and you want to make it stand out.

BOOK SIGNINGS

One of the neatest things about having books carried in a traditional bookstore is the opportunity to have a book signing. Be forewarned, though, that unless you are famous they are not necessarily well attended and you will probably not sell a lot of books. But it is a great way to generate publicity. Best of all, they cost the author very little except in time and travel. If you live in a large city, you will have several local bookstores to choose from. If you have to travel to various towns and cities, keep track of those costs. Keep receipts and log the mileage for your accountant. Whenever possible, do not have a simple book signing, have an event. By this, I mean offer a mini-workshop or or teach a craft or tie it into a theme where people can wear costumes. You can also have a book signing in a specialty store if your topic is relevant. Use your imagination, and it could become an outstanding event.

When you are having a book signing, make sure you confirm the date, time, and address of the bookstore. Take extra copies of your books, a tablecloth that complements your book cover, pens, notepads, tissues, hand lotion, breath mints, and a camera. Make up a name tag so people know you are the author. Bring some things to give away such as bookmarks, photocopied excerpts from the book, a report, and perhaps a dish of candy. Everyone likes a "freebie". You may want to make up labels that say "Signed by author" to place on the cover of any unsold books. Just be sure to actually autograph them. Be pleasant, chatty and witty. Talk to everyone. There are many people who will be shy to approach an author so you have to draw them out. If you are visiting several bookstores in a short time, make up thank you cards in advance for the bookstore owners who host the event. This simple gesture of courtesy will ensure a positive reception if you ever want to come back for another signing.

LIBRARIES

There are more than 21,000 libraries in Canada. That translates into a lot of readers. If your book has been edited and designed professionally, then you have a good chance of selling to libraries. There are university and college libraries out there as well as public libraries, and because of the geographic nature of our vast country, there are a great many regional library systems. What this means for you is that you need only send literature to one source to cover many libraries. To find addresses of all the libraries, look in *Scott's Canadian Source Book*, which you can find in the reference section of your local library.

One of the nice things about libraries is that they usually pay full price for your book. Mind you, they are grateful for any discount because they are often scrambling for funds, and they often reorder when books become damaged or are stolen. This means repeat business. It is amazing that bookstores will return books when libraries will order more. It shows quite a dramatic difference in how they do business. Selling books to libraries can be lucrative if you have the right book.

You will need to approach libraries the way you approach any bookseller with a well done package. Include an information sheet, making sure this one states what formats are available. Libraries also offer audio cassettes and CDs to their readers. If you had extra covers printed they will come in handy now to show what the book looks like. It will also show your back cover blurb, which is one of your best selling features. When it comes to stuffing and addressing envelopes, this is a good time to either belong to a co-operative or start one.

Start with your local branches. They often have budgeted for purchasing books by local authors. Offer to put on an event of some kind to attract attention to your book. Libraries never have enough people volunteering to help, so anything you are prepared to do will be greatly appreciated. Not all libraries purchase books directly, so you may have to deal with library services or any other library wholesaler. Your books will come to the attention of libraries when you register on all the lists and databases I discussed in earlier chapters. If your book subject has longevity, contact the library every couple of years to ask if they need to reorder. Getting your books into libraries can be time consuming for you, but it could pay off handsomely in the end.

WHOLESALERS

A wholesaler is a firm that purchases your books at a 50-55% discount and sells them to booksellers. They are set up to warehouse products, fulfill orders, and deliver books. Some specialize in small or independent publishers. I know it can be shocking to be told that the book you have worked so hard at producing, and spent personal money on, is discounted so highly. But that is the cost of doing business. If you have priced your book properly, you can handle the industry discount. The wholesaler has to be paid too, and must give booksellers their customary 40% or higher discount. Some wholesalers will even promote your book along with the other ones they handle. This makes these companies close to being a distributor. You can find a complete list of wholesalers in *Quill &Quire's Canadian Publishers Directory*.

DISTRIBUTORS

Earlier, I said that many booksellers will not buy books from a self-publisher with only one book. They prefer to deal with one source who can provide many books. A wholesaler can fill that role, but the distributor fills that role and more. Distributors actively market your book. They put out catalogues on a regular basis and have representatives in the field. These reps get to know their booksellers and their needs very well. A distributor can open the door to the large chains and retail outlets. This gets into big business and the average author-publisher is not prepared to do business at that level.

For their services, a distributor receives 60-70% of the purchase price of a book. Their discount is higher than that of a wholesaler because they are actively selling your books within the industry. They attend book fairs, conferences, events, and sell outside Canada. They provide a marketing venue and even guidance to the new publisher. If you are serious about large book sales, you almost have to have a distributor to pull it off. Their names are as respected as the trade publishers and that can be a plus when you are trying to sell books.

All that being said, there is little in the way of distribution for self-publishers in Canada. I can count on one hand the number of distributors I know of that take self-published books. You the publisher have to pay a fee to be included in their catalogue and you have to pay to ship books to their warehouse. You are better to list your books at Amazon.com. Notice I do not say Amazon.ca – you have to have a distributor to be listed on the Canadian site.

BOOK CLUBS

Many writers dream of having their books picked up by a book club, a guarantee of sales beyond your imagination. It is not easy to place books in book clubs, but it is possible. You can find a list of book clubs in Canada by going to **www.bookclubdeals.com.** From there you can see what the various clubs require. Because you have a single book, they might not deal with you directly, so be prepared to find a wholesaler. Remember to have enough books on hand for a book club - do not print 500 books and expect to have enough. You also have to have a great product, so pay attention to the details of designing your book. When you send a promotion package it has so be some of your best marketing literature to date and will need to include a book rather than cover.

FOREIGN SALES

To authors here in Canada, foreign sales

also includes the United States. You will need help to find a market and sell to it. You might want to consider an agent for this since you do not likely have the connections that an agent would. Keep in mind that it might be more cost effective to sell print rights than to sell to many foreign countries, and you definitely need an agent to do that. If you are seriously interested in U.S. sales, you will need a distributor. Even though we have a free trade agreement, it is not simple to sell books across the border. There are customs to clear through and the cost could be prohibitive. Leave this to the experts.

OTHER SALES

You might consider finding a catalogue that your book would be appropriate for. Thousands of catalogues are being printed throughout the year, and these sales are not returnable. If you use one yourself, try starting there. Approach the purchaser with a slick package, and see if you can generate interest. You will need to convince the purchaser why your book would be a great product for their customers. Remember, there is a lot of competition out there. There are catalogues for every type of product you can imagine. To find one that might be right for you, look at the *Catalogue of Canadian Catalogues* available at **Amazon.com.**

Corporate sales can also be lucrative.

If you have a non-fiction book that ties into finance or business practices, you might be able to sell your book to a business or corporation or bank. You might sell a block of non-returnable books to be used either as employee gifts or customer giveaways. If you give seminars based on the material in your book, you might have a product that a corporation would be interested in. When you pitch your book to a corporation, include an autographed copy of the book as well as publicity material with your cover letter. Research the company to target specifically why your book would be worth buying and find the name of the person you should deal with. If you are unsure, try contacting the CEO directly.

Sometimes a book will be suitable to help raise money for your favourite charity. As for catalogues and corporations, you will have to pitch your idea. In this case, though, you donate a portion of sales to the charity rather than sell books outright. An endorsement from the charity can help sell books, because Canadians are supportive of charities. Because Virginia Brucker of British Columbia had lost friends to cancer, she wrote *Gifts From The Heart: 450 Simple Ways to make Your Family's Christmas More Meaningful* to help raise money for the Canadian Cancer Society, who reviewed and endorsed the manuscript before it went to print. The cover informs prospective readers that the purchase of the book helps fund cancer research. Twenty-five percent of the price of each book sold goes to the Cancer Society. Brucker sold the first 2,500 copies in six weeks. This can be a true win-win situation for both the self-publisher and the charity.

CHAPTER EIGHT

Getting Them Out

When a thing is current, it creates currency.
— Marshall McLuhan

FULFILLING ORDERS

Now that you have publicized and marketed your books, you need to be ready for people to purchase them. Orders have to be filled quickly and professionally. If you do not fulfill orders properly, book sales will dry up. Do not think your work is done and that you can now sit back and let the money roll in. You have to send books out to bookstores, library wholesalers and individual customers.

Most of your mail orders will come from either library wholesalers, bookstores or direct customers. When an order arrives, read it carefully. There will be a *purchase order number* on it if it is from a business. You need to quote this on all future correspondence, including invoices. Check that the correct price has been quoted. If you have an ISBN from someone else's list, the orders will go to their place. Check with them frequently so you can get your book or books out in a timely fashion. You should have your books on their way within a week. Depending on which method you choose to ship, it will take time for the order to reach the customer. If you sit on the order too long, you will have an unhappy customer. You are now in the retail business and must endeavour to keep your customers happy at all cost. In our business, we ship orders every Friday via Canada Post.

Unfortunately Canada does not have a mailing rate for books. If your book is no larger than 5.5 x 8.5 and no thicker than half an inch, you can put it into a bubble envelope and it could cost you letter rate depending on the weight. If it is any larger, it will travel as a parcel. In order to help small business, Canada Post has introduced the *VentureOne* card to help save on shipping costs. You receive 5% savings on various types of shipping. Because of this, it is sometimes less expensive to send parcels by the Expedited rate rather than regular. You will also receive $100.00 worth of insurance at no extra cost and a tracking number. To find out more about this program, go to your local post office and speak to someone, or check out their website at **www.canadapost.ca**.

You will need to purchase envelopes to mail your books in. In order to protect the book, buy the ones with the bubbles inside. You can find these at any business supply store. If you order 500 or more, you can often get a deal on the order, so shop around. At the same time you will need to purchase shipping labels. I recommend you use 2"x4" for your outgoing label. They are easy to make up on the computer and are large enough for your logo or other graphic you wish to print on it. Use 1"x2" for your return address labels. That will give you enough room to print your website or e-mail address on it too. These can also be purchased at any business supply store. For larger orders, use brown parcel paper and bubble wrap. I usually place a piece of plain paper between the books so they do not rub on each other and risk damaging the covers. If damaged goods are received by the customer, you are responsible for the postage to have them returned. You then have to pay postage to send out more books. The best advice is to do it right the first time.

Set up a specific place to process and fulfill orders. It might be in your basement, your home office, or even on one end of your dining room table. When you receive the order, read it carefully so you will not make a mistake. If there is something you do not understand, contact the customer who made the order. Make a file folder marked *Pending Orders* and keep orders in there until you get to them. Sometimes this will be a purchase order and sometimes it will be a letter or note from an individual. Fill out an invoice, take a book out of a box, and put the two into a envelope. Whether you choose to print the shipping label before or after this step will not make a difference. Affix postage if you are sending by postal rate. If your book is large enough to be a parcel, take it to the post office or a postal outlet to have it weighed and priced. You do not need to rent a postal metre unless you are selling a substantial number of books.

After you process the order, write the date you sent it out on the order form. This way you will have a record of the order in case it either does not arrive or takes an unusually long time to get there. You do not want word to get out that your orders take a long time to be processed. Mark a file folder marked *Receivables* and move the order into there. When you receive a payment, write the cheque number on both the order form and the invoice, and staple them together. This keeps all documents for each order together. Make another file folder marked *Completed Orders* and put the documents in there. You will keep this until you take it to your accountant at tax time. Afterwards you will archive them. I find that magazine holders make great file folder holders if they are placed long side down. Otherwise, invest in a filing cabinet. An inexpensive two-drawer one will suffice and you can use the extra space to clear up any publishing business clutter that may still be lying around. Whatever you do, though, try not to make filling orders too complex, or you will not enjoy it. Since you are sending out books that are already paid for, you need to take some joy in that.

INVOICES

You can make invoices on your computer. All the word processing programs have templates already made up for you to fill in the blanks. You can also buy an in expensive invoice book and hand write them. The advantage to that is that you have an identical copy. It is easy to forget to print two copies of an invoice if you have little or no business experience. Whichever way you decide to do it, you will need invoices in order to have a paper trail while selling your books.

Your business name, address, phone number, FAX number, e-mail address, and website need to be printed on the invoice. Do not forget to write this information on the top of the blank invoices if you decide to use a pre-printed book. It might be a good investment to have a stamp made up with this information on it. Invoices usually have a space for date, order number, and initials of the person who put the order together. Except for the date, you do not need to fill out the other boxes. Some self-publishers will tell you that you will be identified as a self-publisher if you leave these spaces blank. As long as you are selling books, who cares? There is no shame in self-publishing, and wholesalers and booksellers will buy books from you if they have customers who want them.

When you receive an order from an individual customer, payment should be included if it comes in by mail. The very best way to sell your books is through your website. PayPal makes it possible for small businesses to take payment online. You should set up a PayPal account and have a website to sell your books through.

Not everyone has a credit card though. If you receive an order in the mail with a money order, send the book in a timely fashion because the money order has been prepaid. But you should wait until a cheque clears the bank before processing that order. It might take a week or two before you can ship it, but it is not be worthwhile to go after an individual who sends an NSF cheque for payment. You will have to pay the fees for depositing an NSF cheque, and you may never receive payment from the customer. Be prudent about cheques.

PAYMENT TERMS

Payment terms have changed in the past few years. It used to be acceptable to demand payment in 30 days, but today 60 days is more the norm. Overdue receivables can pose a problem for a small business. Do you let it go 90-120 days or do you charge a penalty after 60 days? If you decide to tack on interest (usually 2% per month), make sure the customer is aware of it. Not that it will make a difference in some cases. Often you will receive the payment after 60 days without the penalty amount added on. The truth is, there is no sense trying to collect it. Some businesses simply do not pay in 60 days and they expect you to go along with that. This kind of business practice is not just found in the publishing sector either. All retail markets are having to put up with it. It seems that retailers are expecting to keep an item on consignment for a couple of months before paying. The attitude is that you should be grateful to have a place to sell your product. This is not a worthwhile battle for an independent publisher to take on. Even the large trade publishers will not do it.

CONSIGNMENT

These days it seems that more and more booksellers want independently published books to be placed in their stores on consignment. That means they do not pay you unless they sell your books. I find this practice appalling. In the regular retail business, goods are purchased at a wholesale price and sold at a retail price. Goods do not go into stores on consignment. By giving standard industry discounts, a bookseller receives your books at a "wholesale" price and sells for retail. Self-publishers have spent many hours hashing out the question of whether to put books out on consignment or not, but it needs discussion here.

The main reason booksellers want your books on consignment is because they do not want to spend either the time or money to start an account for a one-book publisher. The other main reason is that self-published books tend to be poorly designed both inside and out. They do not sell well because of this flaw, so they sit on the shelf a long time. They are also often geared to a select niche market and that makes them harder to sell. While this does not mean that no one will buy your book, it means it will sit on the shelf longer than general books until it finds a market. Small independent booksellers cannot afford to have capital tied up in long term sales. The large chains simply refuse to carry books that they do not believe will sell quickly. In order to get your books into established bookstores, you might not have a choice but to accept a consignment agreement.

A consignment agreement is a contract between you and the bookseller. You need to spell out the terms of the sale. What discount will you give? Since you are not being paid up front, 20-25% is a reasonable discount, although many booksellers still want the industry 40% discount. A big question to have answered is how long the bookseller will carry your books without payment being made. If you have a narrow market, or you have not gathered a reasonable amount of publicity, your book could sit there for a year. That is a long time to have product tied up somewhere and not making money. Three to five months should be the maximum amount of time to keep a book somewhere on consignment. The reality is that if your book is not selling in a particular location, it is time to move it somewhere else. The longer you leave it in the store, the greater the chance of damage by customers who look at it. At some point the book is not worth anything anymore and you will get it back anyway.

The best way to have any chance that a bookseller will actually purchase your books is to make sure they are designed to meet industry standards. This was discussed in detail in Chapters Two and Four. Put together a great marketing package and give the booksellers their discounts, as explained in Chapters Six and Seven. This is how the professionals present their products. They do not have a problem with books being taken on consignment only. Throughout this book I have mentioned the need for professionalism many times. If you want to compete with the trade publishers, you have to be prepared to play by their rules. Packaging and marketing are two major ones. Attention to detail can see your sales to booksellers become a reality.

CHAPTER NINE

More Possibilities

People say we're opportunistic, and I hope
so. I think that's a compliment"
— Samuel Belzberg

AFTERWARD

Now that you are an experienced self-publisher, what can you do next? If you have written non-fiction, you have many possibilities to sell material or spin-offs. You are now viewed as an expert in your field and can use that to start a career in public speaking about your topic. If you are a fiction writer, you can serialize your book. You can also give public readings and become involved with writer's events. It does carry a nice ring to be known as a *novelist* rather than an *author*. Many people aspire to write a novel and the phrase defines you a little more clearly. Whatever you have written, do not stop now that you are published. There are ways to make your material work, and hopefully make money, for you for some time to come.

SELLING RIGHTS

Serialization works well for both fiction and non-fiction. There are two ways to handle it. You can approach magazines and newspapers before you release your book and offer them *first serial rights*. This means you are offering them the right to publish the material for the first time in any publication, including your book. Often the contract will specify "North American" or "Canadian" rights. You will be paid and it will generate a large amount of pre-publicity about your book. The book can be serialized in installments or you can write an excerpt for the publication. It is important that the publication has exclusive rights to the material. They are paying for this and you cannot have it printed in other publications at the same time, including your book. The operative word here is "first".

Second serial rights are basically reprint rights. This material would come out after your book is released. It is not as sought after or well paid, but it is great publicity. Since these rights are non-exclusive, they can be licensed to several publications.

Electronic rights cover everything from online magazines and databases to CD-ROM magazine anthologies and interactive games. Make sure the contract specifies which electronic media are included. Since there is so much controversy about electronic rights, I highly recommend you have any contract looked at by a lawyer before you sign it. Actually, this is a good practice for any contracts within the business. You are not a publishing business expert and need to seek guidance.

Broadcast rights allow your material to be used on the radio. You might even be asked to put together a one or two minute broadcast using your material. While it is a limited source, if your book has enough depth, you should have sufficient material to keep your name in the public realm for a few weeks or months.

Foreign rights are those you sell outside of Canada and can be either *English language* or *translation rights*. If you prefer, you can sell English language reprint rights for a certain territory. This would mean an area such as the Commonwealth or a specific country such as Great Britain. Translation rights will allow the publisher to sell to any country speaking that language. Do not expect to be able to limit the territory, because it would not be lucrative enough for a foreign publisher. To sell foreign rights, it might be prudent to find an agent who is familiar with this aspect of publishing.

Merchandising rights, or licensing rights, means the right to have any commercial reproduction of your words, illustrations, or characters made into merchandise to be sold. This is done in a big way, usually if a character becomes very popular. Merchandise also normally targets the children's audience. If you are a children's writer or an illustrator, investigate this avenue. It can not only give your book longevity, but it can also satisfy the public's hunger for new toys for their children.

ARTICLES

Now that you are considered to be an expert in your field, you can publish articles about your topic for both magazines and newspapers. There are writers in Canada who make a living from the freelance market. Articles can also be "recycled" by changing the slant of the material. Using this time honoured freelancer's trick, you can sell many articles to many different types of publications. Whether you want to go that route or simply bring attention to yourself and your book, there are some rules to follow in the article writing field.

Articles have a fairly defined format. They begin with an *introduction* or "hook" used to peak the reader's interest. The hook can be as short as one sentence or as long as two paragraphs. Right after that comes the *statement* so that the reader understands what the article is about. This is only one or two sentences long. The main part of your article is the *body*. It should be full of anecdotes and information. This is what your reader wants to know. Finish the article with a *resolution* of one or two paragraphs that ties back to the introduction.

When you decide which magazines you want to send articles to, the first things you will need to do is order their guidelines. You can also find guidelines for many publications at **www.writersdigest.com**. Read them carefully so you know what the editor is looking for. If it is apparent you have no idea what the magazine wants, your work will not be accepted. Buy or borrow copies of any that you are interested in and read them. Actually, you should study them to get a feel for the way they want articles written. If you feel that you can emulate their writing style, send a query letter. I will not go into depth about query letters. There are books and courses available to help you write them. If your idea is accepted, take all the guidance from the editor that you can get. You are a book author and will need mentoring until you are better at writing articles.

Never miss a deadline. If you do, your reputation will be destroyed. Those of us who self-publish actually have not had to deal with too many deadlines along the way. That is not how it is when you have an editor to answer to. They expect professionalism, and that means bringing the material in on time.

PUBLIC SPEAKING

Many authors have become successful public speakers. Sometimes they make a good income too. If you are comfortable with speaking in public, you can talk about your subject. You can speak to service clubs, church groups, libraries, professional organizations, or civic groups. With determination and imagination, you could set up a speaking circuit that would keep you busy for some time. Whenever there is an opportunity, try to have the media cover your lecture for further publicity.

You want to be prepared when you give public talks. The most obvious thing is to have enough books on hand. It is better to bring too many than to run out. Write an introduction for the person who will be introducing you. That way it is accurate. You will also want to have a poster of your book so it is visible even to the people in the back of the room. Do not forget to bring any marketing material such as bookmarks or postcards. You might also want to make up fliers with order forms in case someone is not sure if they are ready to make a purchase. Do not pressure customers. They will appreciate being given time to think about buying. This might even end up in multiple purchases. Bring change and, if you take credit cards, bring the machine and slips. Many times, you will sell more than one book to a customer if you can accept a credit card. If you are speaking in another town or city, make sure the local bookstores carry your book so it is available after you have gone.

WORKSHOPS AND SEMINARS

Once you have written and published a book, you can use it as a platform to begin teaching about your topic. I conduct workshops about self-publishing and how to get published. These day-long workshops give me an opportunity to introduce self-publishing to people, meet some of my readers, and add to my bank account. I am comfortable teaching and have training in that area.

When you prepare for a workshop or seminar, you first have to develop an outline. This allows you to see visually what material you want to cover. You may find it is either too much or too little for the time you are allowed. If it is too much, consider a narrower aspect of your topic. If it is too little, go back to your book to find more material to "flesh it out". Having your workshop outlined will make it easier for you to organize both your material and any resources you will need. You will need to invest in a laptop computer and a projector. The days of using a chalkboard or even an overhead projector are pretty much over. Prepare a PowerPoint presentation and learn to use it before testing it out on a classroom full of students. If you are not well prepared, your audience will have doubts about your ability and that will raise doubts about your knowledge. A good workshop presenter should exude a sense of assurance. After all, if you are now the "expert" on the subject, you should be able to present it with confidence.

Beforehand, contact the facility where you are giving your workshop or seminar to make sure you know where the room is and who will let you in the building. Make sure the coordinator is clear about what you need in the room such as chairs and tables. If there is going to be coffee and tea available, find out who supplies it. Well in advance, give the facility coordinator all material you require to have photocopied, and make sure you write down clearly how many copies you will need. We often conduct workshops in the evening or on a weekend and the staff who do the photocopying do not usually work at those times. Planning ahead is an important part of being organized. If you are presenting your workshop in a non-educational venue, you have to make your own photocopies. Keep a master so you do not have to sort through the material every time you teach it.

I prefer to use a three-column table format for my outline. The first column gives the main teaching points, the second column covers information I want to remember to present, and the third column is for notes where I might list my handouts and any aids I want to show the students. I also use it to make notes and jot down student questions. You can find many books on the subject of giving workshops and seminars, and you can subscribe to online newsletters. It is not difficult, though, if you plan ahead and organize everything. After your first workshop or seminar, you will want to make some changes to the material or format. This will only perfect your presentation and draw larger groups to hear it.

BOOKLETS AND REPORTS

These are also called "spin-offs" and can generate a lot of income for the non-fiction writer. You could even make a living selling booklets. There are actually people who do. Because you are the expert, and you wrote the book, you can market any part or piece of it that you wish. Remember, you own the copyright and it is not plagiarism if you use your own text word for word.

Typical booklets are short, from five to sixty-four pages. They can be printed on a high speed photocopier and stapled at the fold. They are not intended to ever sit on a bookstore shelf, so you do not need to worry about a spine. The cover can be made from card stock. They are used to either give more detailed information about a segment of your material or condense something that is very detailed.

A report is short and printed on 8 ½" x 11" paper. A report with more than one sheet, can be stapled at the corner. It can be a resource list or detailed bibliography or a kit or just about anything that you think a reader might want to have more information about. Letters and requests from your fans can point you in the direction of what materials might be turned into a good report. You can mail these folded in #10 envelopes with a first class stamp.

Booklets and reports can be advertised in the back of your book, on your website, or in the classified section of periodicals that relate to the topic of your book. They can be sold as direct sales which I explained in Chapter Seven or be given away. If you plan to send it free of charge, you can do it one of three ways. One way is to request a self-addressed stamped envelope (SASE) in order to defray your costs. Another way is to offer it as a free download from your website. This is becoming more popular and the cost to you is pretty much nil. You can also use it as a promotional item. Offer it for free if the customer purchases your book (or a certain number of them) or fills out an online form. The latter will allow you to build a database for future marketing. Booklets can become a serious part of your publishing business.

AWARDS

Nothing makes your book stand out more than winning an award. You become instantly well-known in Canadian literary circles, and your books will each carry a sticker announcing the win. Sales will increase because people always want to read award winning books.

Unfortunately most self-published books do not qualify for the majority of awards. This is primarily because the quality of self-published books has been so poor. Award committees want professionally designed and printed books and they know that the trade publishers do that.

The first thing you need to do is go to the website or write to the organization and ensure your book is suitable for entry. Send the book or books with a self-addressed and stamped post card requesting receipt information so you know it has arrived safely. I cannot stress enough the importance of reading entry guidelines thoroughly. Here is that professional angle I have talked about before. If you miss out on something, you will be viewed as a self-published amateur. This is not good publicity for either yourself or others.

Writer's Digest magazine runs the Annual International Self-Published Book Awards every year. There is a grand prize winner and several categories to choose from. While it does cost a fee to submit a book, the grand prize is well worth the cost. There are also Category winners and all winners will also receive book jacket seals along with promotion on the magazine's website. All honourable mentions are listed in an edition of the magazine when they announce the winners. It is not cheap to enter, but offers an opportunity to have your book read by a serious editor. If you win anything, the cost of entry then becomes moot.

TRADE PUBLISHERS

Once you have successfully self-published a book, trade publishers will find you more interesting. If you would rather have someone else publish your books in the future, you are now considered a reasonable risk. After all, you did it once and proved that you are capable of writing a book from start to finish. You now have a "name" and are no longer a complete unknown. You understand the publishing business and will be able to help, rather than hinder, your publishing house's attempts to market your book. If you made the rounds and received either silence or rejection slips, this could very well be your "calling card" to finding a publisher receptive to your next manuscript.

The other side of the coin is if your book is so wildly successful, and you cannot keep up with print runs, you want to find a publisher to buy the rights to publish your book. If this happens, you will be famous and making a lot of money. You can make a deal with the trade publisher that will give you a larger royalty than the average author makes. Or you can partner with a publisher to co-publish the book. This will require an extensive contract which will need to be seen by a lawyer.

REMAINDERS

Sometimes a book does not sell well and other times it simply runs its course. When you find that you have been storing boxes of books for a few years, it might be time to investigate the remainders market. If you have ever been to a bookstore with older but unused books, they are probably remainders. Remainder sellers often show up in malls with tables of books. Try not to think of the remainder market as the demise of your book. It is actually a way to give new life to an old product.

Remainders dealers throughout North America receive at least a 70-80% discount. This may mean you receive only the cost of producing the book. That is better than receiving nothing. It is definitely better than storing hundreds, or even thousands, of books in your basement or garage. Remember, this is a product and needs to be moved out. If you plan to write and publish another book, you will need the room. If you are tired of the whole project, you do not really want it staring at you day after day. If you are prepared to put your business hat on, you will see that sending books off to a remainders dealer is simply a good business decision. Not that you have to, of course. You may want to keep all of your books and continue to sell them for the rest of your life. They belong to you and you can do whatever you want to do with them. But it is nice to know that if you do not want to store them anymore, there is an avenue for sales.

CHAPTER TEN

Success Stories

*You are born with two things: existence
and opportunity , and these are the raw
materials out of which you can make
a successful life.*
— Charles Templeton

We often believe that good things
will never happen to us. We think that only
"others" will win the lottery or find a business
that makes them rich. This chapter is about
average people, like you and me, who found
a niche and worked hard to make their books
into best sellers. Admittedly, they are all non-
fiction books, but with the upsurge in self-
publishing, it will not be long before we see
more fiction hitting the bestseller lists.

Studying successful people is one way to
understand how they got that way. That is why
biographies and autobiographies of the rich

and famous sell so well. It is human nature to also want to be wildly successful. We wonder if we emulate them, will we also have success. I have touched on some of the most successful self-publishers in Canada. To learn more about the people and their achievements, visit their websites.

Jean Paré
Books: *Company's Coming* cookbooks series
Number sold: 30 million+
Website: **www.companyscoming.com**

The most successful self-publisher in Canada, Jean Paré was an Alberta caterer who merely tried to fill a gap for requests for some of her recipes. She published *150 Delicious Squares* and travelled through the province to find retailers to take them, delivering them from the trunk of her car. As more people wanted more recipes, she wrote more cookbooks. Today the *Company's Coming* series has more 30 million books in print. Total sales have surpassed $20 million. The company she co-founded with her son-in-law is operated by family members, which gave Jean Paré plenty of time to work with the staff in the test kitchen. She retired this year after thirty years publishing cookbooks.

David Chilton
Book: *The Wealthy Barber*

Number of book sold: 3 million+
Website: **www.wealthybarber.com**

Dave Chilton started by hiring a consulting firm to help him prepare the book - and he wisely followed their advice. He took a year off work to travel and promote his book. Self-published in his basement, he sold 12,000 copies in the first two months alone. He is a shrewd businessman who made smart deals with publishers and corporations. According to one report, he believes in the need for an order form at the back of the book. He discovered that people actually order more books when there is one. He took this self-publishing business seriously and it made him into the successful author and speaker he is today. He has a sequel coming out in the fall of 2011.

Greta and Janet Podleski
Book: *Looney Spoons: Low-fat made fun!*
Number sold: 850,000+
Book: *CrazyPlates: Low-fat food so good, you'll swear it's bad for you!*
Number sold: 500,000+
Book: *Eat, Shrink & Be Merry!*
Website: **www.eatshrinkandbemerry.com**

Ontario sisters, Janet and Greta Podleski, are a determined pair of women. They believed so strongly in their funny approach to a low-fat cookbook that they put everything they had into getting it published. Greta moved in with Janet and her husband, they quit their jobs and maxed out their credit cards. They even sold many of their possessions to raise the money to make this project work. The story of selling Janet's car at a lawn sale is a true one.

David Chilton invested in the book and put his well honed marketing skills behind it. The rest, as they say, is history. After one appearance on *The Today Show*, their book was #1 on Ingram's cookbook bestseller list. Today the partners have seen successful with a second cookbook which was a national #1 bestseller and a 2001 finalist for the James Beard Foundation Cookbook awards. When their third cookbook came out, they were given a show on Food Network television.

Dania Lebovics

Books: *Kiddy Chronicles* (no longer available)
       Baby Chronicles (in its 14th printing)
       School Year Chronicles
       High School Chronicles
       Baby Chronicles Pregnancy Planner
Number sold: 100,000+
Website: **www.babychronicles.com**

Dania Lebovics made her first *Kiddy Chronicles* for herself to chronicle the events in her child's life. She made some as gifts for friends, and then phone calls started coming from people who had seen them and wanted one. Her first three editions were designed on her home computer and printed at the local copy shop. She had them bound professionally and placed on consignment in baby and maternity stores. She used up the family savings and then decided to take a chance on future editions. This chance paid off and her book was even featured on the television show Two and a Half Men.

Virginia Brucker
Book: *Gifts From the Heart: 450 Simple Ways to Make Your Family's Christmas More Meaningful*
Number sold: 27,000+
Website: **www.webelieve.ca**

When cancer struck a staff member and the parents of two students at a small British Columbia school, teacher Virginia Brucker believed she had to do something. What she did was create a book with imaginative ways to celebrate the Christmas season without spending a lot of money. She wanted to use the book as a way to raise money for the Canadian Cancer Society. With the help of school staff and students, she had the book ready to go in three years. Even the cover artwork came from a 10-year-old student.

Available mainly online, by phone or mail, twenty-five percent of the profits are donated to the Cancer Society. Groups that use the book for a fundraiser receive another forty percent. So far, more than $98,500 has been donated to the Cancer Society. *Gifts From the Heart* has been written about in the *Ottawa Citizen* and *Canadian Living* magazine. The Canadian Centre for Philanthropy published a whole page praising the author and her husband for their dedication and volunteer work. *Gifts from the Heart* was picked up by a trade publisher in 2006.

Joe Garner

Books: *Never Fly Over An Eagle's Nest*
      Never A Time To Trust
      Never Chop Your Rope
      Never Under The Table
      Never Forget The Good Times
Number sold: approximately 300,000+

The late Joe Garner's success was due primarily to his tenacity as a salesman. At the age of 71, the British Columbia writer self-published his first book, and it went on to sell more than 100,000 copies over the next 15 years. He packed his van with 1,500 copies and drove across Canada selling them along the way. He spoke at libraries, in bookstores, on the radio, and at every service club that would have him. He was so successful that he even had to have more books printed and shipped to him in Calgary on the way back. Beating the odds, his second book also became a bestseller. He started his final book at the age of 84. Even though he suffered a stroke while writing it, he continued to work on it. He wrote books because he wanted to tell his stories and give his readers pleasure. He even once admitted that writing was part of what kept him alive.

THE ENTREPRENEURIAL SPIRIT

One of the main things you will learn from reading about these successful self-publishers is that they have tenacity and courage. It takes a lot of courage to quit your job or take a long leave of absence. It takes courage to clean out the family's savings account, max out credit cards, or remortgage your home. It takes courage to start any kind of business, much less a self-publishing one. And it takes an incredible amount of courage to give interviews and speak publicly about your book. All these successful self-publishers possess a rare courage that has allowed them to follow this dream.

Something all of these authors have in common is that they were willing to "bang the drum" about their book. They toured and they spoke and they interviewed and they did whatever it took to bring their books to the attention of the buying public. Along the way, you can be sure they made mistakes. But they learned from their mistakes and kept right on going. This is the true entrepreneurial spirit.

Self-publishing is both demanding and gratifying. It is time consuming, costs money, and has its own idiosyncrasies. It is easy to print a book, but more complex to market one. It takes guts and determination. None of Canada's successful self-publishers fell into success. They made it themselves. You can achieve success too, if you have the right product and a positive attitude. I wish every one of you good luck in your publishing endeavours. Make use of the resources I have listed in the appendices and visit my website at **www.selfpublishing.ca** for great links and current information. Maybe a future edition of this book will feature you and your book as a success story.

CHECKLIST

To Do	Done	Date
Write the book		
Have the manuscript edited		
Proofread manuscript and make corrections		
Choose a publication date		
Choose a business name		
Register the business		
Open business account at bank		
Research Books in Print for a title		
Choose a title		
Design the cover		
Write back cover material		
Order ISBN		
Order Cataloging in Publication (CIP) information		
Complete New Books Service form		
Order a bar code		
Register with BowkerLink		
Have book formatted		
Organize illustrations and write cutlines		
Get printer estimates		
Write a marketing plan		
Write blurbs of various lengths		
Write an information sheet		

Write news release		
Make up media package		
Put up website		
Have books printed		
Send book(s) to Legal Deposit		
Re-read Chapter 7 and sell books		

REQUEST FOR QUOTATION
Half Acre Publishing
3321 Renita Ridge Road Duncan BC V9L 5J6
Phone/FAX 250-746-3919 halfacre@selfpublishing.ca
www.selfpublishing.ca

BOOK TITLE: Self Publishing in Canada: A complete guide to designing, printing and selling your book – Second Edition
QUANTITY: prices for 1000/1500
TOTAL PAGES: 265
TRIM SIZE (Includes front and back material): 5.5" x 8.5"
PAPER: TEXT: 60#
                COVER: 12 pt
ARTWORK: 4 line illustrations - no photos
COVER: 4 colour
BINDING: Perfect binding with laminate
FORMAT: Disk or PDF
FEE FOR EXTRA PAPER COVERS:
PACKAGING:
SHIPPING CHARGE:
DELIVERY DATE:
RE-ORDER TURNAROUND TIME:
DROP SHIP CHARGE:
        MINIMUM NUMBER:
TERMS:
Over/under run not to exceed 10%.
Boards, flats, and all artwork will be returned to the customer upon completion of project.

This quote good for ___14_____ days from date shown below.

Signed _____

Date _____

ASSOCIATIONS FOR WRITERS

Association of Canadian Publishers
www.publishers.ca

Canadian Authors Association
www.canauthors.org

Canadian Federation of Poets
www.federationofpoets.com

Canadian Poetry Association
www.canadianpoetryassociation.webs.com

Canadian Society of Children's Authors,
Illustrators & Performers (CANSCAIP)
www.canscaip.org

Crime Writers of Canada
www.crimewriterscanada.com

Federation of British Columbia Writers
www.bcwriters.com

Independent Publishers Association of
Canada
www.ipac-calgary.com

Inscribe Christian Writers' Fellowship
www.inscribe.org

Island Writers Association (PEI)
www.peiwritersguild.wordpress.com

League of Canadian Poets
www.poets.ca

Manitoba Writers' Guild Inc.
www.mbwriter.mb.ca

The Ontario Poetry Society
www.theontariopoetrysociety.ca

PEN Canada
www.pencanada.ca

Periodical Writers Association of Canada
www.pwac.ca

Professional Editors Association
www.editors.ca

Professional Editors Association of Vancouver
Island
www.peavi.bc.ca

Quebec Writers' Federation
www.qwf.org

Alberta Romance Writers' Association
www.albertaromancewriters.com

Romance Writers of America - Greater Vancouver Chapter
www.rwagvc.com

Romance Writers of America - Vancouver Island Chapter
www.vicrwa.ca

Saskatchewan Writers' Guild
www.skwriter.com

SFCanada (Science Fiction Writers)
www.sfcanada.ca

Writers' Alliance of Newfoundland and Labrador
www.writersalliance.nf.ca

The Writers' Federation of New Brunswick
www.umce.ca/wfnb/

Writers' Federation of Nova Scotia
www.writers.ns.ca

Writers Guild of Alberta
www.writersguild.ab.ca

Writers Guild of Canada
www.writersguildofcanada.com

Writers' Union of Canada
www.writersunion.ca

WEBSITES FOR WRITERS AND PUBLISHERS

Booksellers
www.amazon.com
www.authographedbyauthor.com
www.booksamillion.com
www.booksatoz.com
www.cyclopsmedia.com
www.ebookmall.com
www.justbookz.com
www.knowbetter.com
www.lights.com/publisher/ca.html
www.selfpublishingservice.com

Distributors
www.redtuquebooks.ca
* Red Tuque Books National Distributor
White Knight Book Distribution Services Ltd
(no website)

General Information and Resources
www.authorlink.com
www.author.co.uk
* Self-publishing site in the UK
www.bookwire.com
* Maintained by R.R. Bowker
www.cbabook.org
* Canadian Booksellers Association
www.cla.ca
* Canadian Library Association

www.parapub.com
- Dan Poynter's site

www.published.com

www.pma-online
- Publishers Marketing Association

www.rtir.com

www.selfpublishing.ca
- Self Publishing in Canada

www.sfwa.org/beware

www.spannet.org
- Small Publishers Association of North America

www.spawn.org
- Small Publishers, Artists, and Writers Network

www.strategis.ic.gc.ca

www.talion.com/presskits.html

Marketing

www.authorsden.com

www.bookbooters.com

www.bookclubdeals.com

www.bookmarket.com

www.publicizeyourbook.com

www.publishinggame.com

www.umbrellabooks.com

Newsletters and magazines

www.bcbookworld.com
- Canada's largest circulation newspaper about books

www.forewordmagzine.com

www.independentpublisher.com
www.publishingbasics.com
www.quillandquire.com
  • Canada's publishing periodical
www.wexfordpress.com/news/news2.pdf
www.worldwidewriters.com
www.writersdigest.com
  • Articles, a newsletter, and a large
  database of publisher's guidelines.
www.writepage.com

GLOSSARY OF PUBLISHING TERMS

A

AA Author's Alterations, the changes made by the author on proofs. Can be costly to the author if there are too many changes.

ABI Advanced Book Information. Publishers supply R.R. Bowker with information about their book which is used to list books in *Forthcoming Books* and *Books in Print*. They prefer you register online, but you can still use the form.

Acid-free paper Paper which will not yellow and will not deteriorate for two hundred years.

Acknowledgment A statement expressing gratitude for contributions to a work by an individual or organization. Part of the book's FRONT MATTER.

Acquisition librarian The librarian who chooses and orders new library books.

Adoptions Books accepted for use as textbooks in schools, colleges, and universities.

Advance An agreed prepayment to the author, paid either before or at the time of publication, to be offset against future royalties.

Advance copies Copies of a publication made up in limited quantity for promotional purposes.

Afterword The author's final remarks to the reader. Part of the book's AFTER MATTER.

AKA "also known as" or an alias. See Pen

name and Pseudonym.

Anthology A collection of writings by one or more authors published as a single book.

Appendix A list of resources or other reference material. Part of a book's AFTER MATTER. Plural form is appendices.

Artwork Any illustrative matter such as photographs, illustrations, charts or graphs other than straight text.

As-told-to A book produced by a writer in collaboration with a non writer, usually a celebrity.

B

Back jacket flap The back inner flap of a dust jacket that often has an author's biography and sometimes a photo.

Backlist Previously published books that are still in print and available from the publisher.

Back matter All pages in a book after the main text such as APPENDICES, GLOSSARY, BIBLIOGRAPHY, or INDEX. Also called END MATTER.

Back order An order for books held until they become available.

Bar code The ISBN and price code that is on the back cover of the book. Called the Bookland 13 EAN.

Bastard title Half title page that is the first page of a book.

Bestseller A top selling book based on bookstore sales.

Biblio A page in the front matter of a book giving details of the publisher and publishing history. Also called the legal page.

Bibliography List of publications providing reference material on the book's subject. Part of the BACK MATTER.

Binding Method of securing the leaves or signatures of a book, brochure or manuscript.

Blank An unprinted page that is part of a signature.

Bleed The part of an image that extends beyond the trim marks on a page.

Blue pencil A special pencil whose marks cannot be reproduced, used to make corrections on camera-ready copy.

Blurb A promotional advertisement, announcement or phrase.

Boards Stiff paper in the cover of a hardback book or the camera-ready pasted up copy ready for the printer.

Body The text portion of a book excluding FRONT MATTER and BACK MATTER.

Boldface Type with a heavy, black appearance.

Book A publication of 49 or more pages that is not a serial or periodical.

Bookfair An event where publishers display and sell their books.

Booklet A publication with more pages than pamphlet and less than a book, usually fewer than 24 pages long.

Book proofs Page proofs put together in a book form.

Bulk Both the thickness of a sheet of paper and the thickness of a book without its cover.

C

CIS Coated One Side. Refers to a book cover stock which is smooth and shiny on one side.

Camera-ready Artwork, copy, or pasteup that is ready to be photographed without alteration.

Caps Capital or uppercase letters.

Caption Descriptive text accompanying an illustration, drawing, table, etc.

Cased/case-bound Hardcover book.

Casting off Calculating the number of typeset pages based on character count.

Chapbook A small book or pamphlet of ballads, poems or popular tales.

Character A single letter, number, punctuation mark, or space.

CIP Cataloging in Publication. A voluntary program, run by the National Library of Canada, whereby Canadian books are catalogued before they are published and the cataloging information is distributed to librarians and booksellers.

Clip art Pictures that can be purchased and used in books and other publications.

Clipping service A firm that collects articles, reviews and notices for a fee.

Cloth A material used for casing books.

Coated paper Paper stock with a white clay surface for smooth printing.

Collating Gathering sheets together in proper order.

Colour correction Any method used to improve colour rendition such as masking, dot etching and scanning.

Colour printing Any print colour except black on white paper.

Colour separation Camera technique of separating each of the four primary colours for the four necessary printing plates.

Comb binding A plastic multi-pronged binding that allows a book to lie flat.

Composition The process of setting type.

Concordance The list of primary words, names, or terms that form the foundation of a computerized index.

Condensed A more compact version of typeface.

Content editing The process of evaluating a manuscript for style, organization and large general revisions.

Co-op Where a group of people share the costs of such items as advertising or publishing.

Copy The text of a book.

Copy editing Technical editing of a manuscript for spelling, grammar, punctuation and consistency.

Copyright The right of a person to retain or sell copies of artistic works that they have produced.

Copyright infringement Unauthorized and illegal use of copyrighted material.

Copyright notice A notice that protects publicly distributed information and must include the symbol and the word "copyright".

Cropping Placing pencil marks at the margins and corners to indicate what portion of a photo or illustration is to be omitted.

Cross reference A reference made from one part of a book to another.

Cutline Another term for caption.

D

Database A collection of data stored in the computer's memory in such a way that it can be retrieved in a different order if required.

Dedication Inscription honouring the person or persons who inspired the book. Part of the FRONT MATTER.

Demographics A profile of a group based on such criteria as age, sex, marital status, education, and socioeconomic level, useful in marketing.

Desktop publishing Near typeset quality and printed publications done with a computer.

Die cut The creation of openings, shapes or folds by cutting away part of the paper stock.

Direct mail Promotional material mailed directly to potential customers.

Display ad A print advertisement that is larger than a classified ad.

Display type Larger or boldface type for heads, subheads, etc.

Drop cap A large capital letter dropped into

text at the beginning of a line; can be used at the beginning of a chapter.

Dummy A rough layout of how the finished book is to appear.

Duotone A process for producing an illustration in two colours from a one colour original.

Dust cover The paper wrapper that goes around the cover of a hardcover but is not stuck on. Also called a *dust jacket*.

E

Editing Making or suggesting changes in a manuscript.

Edition One or more printings of a work that are basically the same. Can be a revised edition or limited edition.

E-publishing Publishing a book in a format readable by a computer or specialized reader.

Em Unit of typographical and linear measurement based on the capital letter "M".

En A measurement used in casting off equivalent to half an "M".

Endpapers The leaves of paper at the front and end of a book which cover the inner sides of the boards securing the book to its case.

Engraving The design or lettering etched on a plate or block.

Enlargement Photographic process of creating an image larger than the original.

Epilogue A concluding section that rounds out a story and often updates the reader.

Errata Errors found after the book is printed.

Excerpt A portion taken from a longer work. Also called an Extract.

Exclusive A news or feature story printed by one source ahead of its competitors.

F

Face Short for *typeface*. In computer terms it is called the font.

Facing page Any page forming a double spread with another as seen when the book is open.

Fair use The allowable and legal use of a limited amount of copyrighted material without getting permission.

First serial rights The right to serialize a printed work prior to publication.

Flap That part of the jacket of a hardcover book that is folded so as to lie between the paper and the front and back cover.

Flap copy The text describing the book and the author which appear on the inside flap of hardcover books.

Flat fee A negotiated set fee that an author or illustrator receives for a job of work.

Flier Inexpensive advertising printed on 8 ½ x 11 paper.

F.O.B. Free on Board. It means the quoted price does not include delivery costs.

F and Gs Folded and gathered pages. Sheets that have been folded and collated but not finally trimmed or sewn, sent to the publisher for approval before printing begins.

Folio The page number printed on text pages.

Font Computer terminology for typeface.

Foreign rights Subsidiary rights allowing a work to be published in another country or in other languages.

Foreword Introductory remarks by someone other than the author about the book, subject and its author. Part of the book's FRONT MATTER.

Format The general style or appearance of a book.

Formatting The process of designing a publication.

Freelancer Someone who is self-employed and sells their writing, artistic or editing services on a contract basis to publishers.

Front matter The pages preceding the body of a book. Also called PRELIMS.

Frontispiece An illustration facing the title page. Also called front plate.

Fulfillment Filling and shipping book orders.

G

Galleys Proofs from the typesetter before the copy has been divided into pages.

Gathering Placing the sections of a book in the correct order for binding.

Genre A category of writing such as science fiction, mystery, romance, etc.

Ghostwriting Writing a book in conjunction with someone else as if it had been written by that other person.

Glossary List giving definitions of terms

related to a particular subject. Part of the BACK MATTER.

Glossy A photograph with a shiny finish rather than a matte finish.

Graphics Illustrations other than photographs.

Gutter The inside centre margins of a book.

Gutter bleed An image allowed to extend unbroken across the central margins of a spread.

H

Half-title A page with the title and publisher's name only printed on it that immediately precedes the title page.

Halftone Process by which continuous tone of photographs is simulated by a pattern of dots of varying sizes.

Hanging indent Form of typesetting in which the initial line of each paragraph is set full measure and the remaining lines are indented.

Hardcover book A cased book with a board cover.

Head The margin at the top of a page.

Heading The title introducing a chapter.

House style The style of spelling, punctuation and spacing used in a printing or publishing house to ensure consistency.

I

Illustrations Photographs, drawings, graphs

and tables used in a book to explain or supplement the text.

Image area Amount of space given to a particular image in design and printing.

Impression All copies of a book printed at the same time from the same type or plates.

Imprint The name of the publisher including place and date of publication.

In print Books and other publications that are currently available from the publisher.

Index The section of a publication giving alphabetical listing of subject, proper names, etc. mentioned in the book with page references.

ISBN International Standard Book Number.

J

Justify To space out lines of type so that both margins are aligned.

K

Kerning To adjust the space between selected pairs of characters.

L

Lamination A glossy coating for book covers that protect against scuffing and keeps covers from curling.

Layout The design for how the printed material, including illustrations, will look.

Leading The space added between lines of type.

Leaf In a book, a single sheet of paper comprised of one page printed on each side.

Legal page The page carrying the details of printing, copyright, etc. Also called biblio. Found in the FRONT MATTER.

Libel Written defamation of character.

Ligature Certain letters traditionally joined to form a single character.

Limited edition A limited quantity of books printed.

Line copy or line art Solid black and white copy for reproduction.

List All the titles a publisher has in print and for sale.

List price The retail price of a book before discount.

Lowercase The uncapitalized letters of a typeface.

M

Manuscript A book before it is typeset and printed. Abbreviated as Mss.

Margin The white space that surrounds the text on a page.

Markup The process of marking a manuscript with directions for the typesetter.

Mass-market paperback The small paperbacks designed for mass market sales.

Master Original camera ready artwork.

Measure The width of a full line of type, usually measured in points and picas.

Model release A form giving permission to use a photo of a person in your publication.

N

Net receipt Money received by the publisher after discounts.

News release A one page story about the author or book or books's subject sent to media for promotion.

Notched binding A type of adhesive binding in which the untrimmed spin is notched and roughened before being force fed with glue.

O

Offset printing The transfer of an inked image to paper using a rubber blanket.

Opaque To paint portions of a negative so it cannot reproduce.

Out of print A book that is no longer available because the publisher has none left in print.

Orphan The first line of a new paragraph that appears by itself at the bottom of a page.

Overrun The extra number of books the printer may produce, and should not exceed 10%.

P

Pagination Numbering, in order, the pages of a book.

Paperback A softcover book with a paper cover.

Paste up The camera ready original prepared for offset printing.

PDF Portable Document Format is a universal file format developed by Adobe® that preserves all the fonts, formatting, graphics, and colour of any source document, regardless of the application and platform used to create it. You will find PDF a very common format which is widely used on the internet due to its platform independence.

PE Printer's error, used in correcting a proof.

Pen name A pseudonym used to conceal the author's real name.

Perfect binding A squared spine made by gluing the ends together.

Permission Authorization from a copyright holder to quote material.

Pica A typographic measurement equal to 12 points. Six picas equal one inch.

Plagiarism Copying another author's work and taking credit for it as your own.

Plastic binding A type of binding using a plastic spiral or comb.

Plate The printing master containing the image to be printed.

Point A typographic measurement equal to 1/72 inch.

Point of purchase display Book racks, bookmarks, posters, and other sales material given to booksellers to promote the book.

PPI Pages Per Inch is used to describe thickness of paper stock.

Preface Introductory remarks written by the author. Part of the FRONT MATTER.

Prelims The pages of a book that you have before the actual text or body begins. Also called Front Matter.

Prepack Point of purchase countertop or floor display made of cardboard and filled with your books.

Press kit Publicity materials in presentation folder sent to the media.

Press release Also called a news release.

Print run The number of copies of a book printed at one time. Also called a press run.

Promotional material Any printed matter that promotes the book.

Proof A page of text or photographs that shows what the end product will look like.

Pseudonym A pen name.

Publication date The date when a book is officially considered available for purchase.

Public domain Material that is not protected by copyright.

Q

Quote Exact copy of copyrighted original wording from another source, and enclosed in quotation marks.

R

Recto The right hand page of a book.

Remainders Leftover books that are sold for a fraction of their cost.

Reprint A new printing of a book.

Retouching Touch up a photograph to correct flaws.

Returns Books that have not been sold are returned to the publisher for a refund or credit.

Review An evaluation of a book made available to the public.

Review copy A complimentary copy of a book sent to a reviewer.

Revised edition A new edition of a book containing substantial new or updated material.

Rights The various rights to publish a work in any form.

Running head Copy set at the tops of printed pages outside the text area and can include book name, chapter name or author name. Will include page number.

S

Saddle stitching Binding a book by driving staples through the fold at the centre.

Sans serif A letter or typeface without serifs as in sans serif.

SASE Self addressed stamped envelope.

Second serial rights The rights for a magazine to run an excerpt after the publication date.

Self cover A cover for a pamphlet, etc. made of the same paper as the text pages.

Serif The short ending stroke of a character in a typeface.

Short run A small print job of less than 500 books.

Shrink wrap Clear plastic wrap used to keep books from being damaged while shipping. books.

Signature The multiples of pages that books

are printed in for offset printing.

Simultaneous editions Releasing both hard cover and soft cover at the same time.

Sinkage The space from the top margin of a text page to the first printed element on the page.

Slipcase A protective box in which a set of books is placed with the spines facing outward.

Small caps Capital letters the same height as lower case letters.

Smythe sewn Signatures are sewn together before the hard cover is glued on.

Spine The back of a book binding.

Spine out When a book is displayed on a shelf so that the spine faces out.

Spiral binding A continuous wire binding threaded through holes punched near the back margin.

Stock Paper used for printing or binding.

Style sheet A guide for editorial or typographic decisions used to ensure consistency.

Subsidiary rights Additional rights that can be sold in addition to the book.

Subsidy publisher A company that charges writers to print their book and puts its own ISBN on the legal page thereby owning the book.

Subtitle An additional title usually used to clarify the actual subject of a non-fiction book.

T

Table of contents A list in the PRELIM that gives the name of chapters and what page number they start on.

Table of illustrations A list in the PRELIM that notes illustrations and what page they are on.

Tail margin The bottom margin on a page.

Tear sheets Newspaper or magazine reviews, ads or articles cut or torn out.

Terms The number of days before the customer must pay an invoice.

Text The main body of type.

Titles Refers to all books the publisher has in print.

Title page The recto page that gives the book's title/subtitle, author, publisher, and place and date of publication.

Trade paperback A larger paperback.

Trade publisher Commercial publishing house that typically pays authors a royalty to publish and sell their book.

Trim size The dimensions of a full page including the margins, given in inches.

Typeface The style characteristics of a complete font type which usually has a name.

Type styles Type characteristics of a more general kind than those of the various typefaces.

Typographer A type designer or someone who sets type.

U

Underrun When the printer makes less copies than were ordered.

Unit cost The cost of each book after all expenses have been taken into consideration.

Uppercase The capital letters of a typeface.

V

Vanity press Old fashioned term for subsidy publisher.

Varnish A shiny protective coating applied to a book's cover.

Velo binding A fused plastic binding.

Verso A left hand page.

W

Web press A printing press that uses roll fed paper rather than sheets.

Wholesaler A company who buys from a publisher and resells to booksellers.

Widow The last line of a paragraph that appears alone at the top of a new page.

Working title The title of a book used while it is being written.

X

x-height The height of the lowercase letter "x" in a particular typeface.

BIBLIOGRAPHY

Anderson, Scott, ed. *The Book Trade in Canada: Your complete guide to the Canadian publishing marketplace.* 1998 ed. Toronto: Quill & Quire, 1998

Applebaum, Judith. *How To Get Happily Published 5th ed.* New York: HarperPerennial, Publishers Inc, 2002

Bates, Jem. *The Canadian Writer's Market.* Toronto: McClelland & Stewart Inc, 1996

Brucker, Virgina. *Your Marketing Plan.* Nanoose Bay, BC: We Believe Publications, 2003

The Chicago Manual of Style: The Essential Guide for Writers, Editors, and Publishers. 14th ed. Chicago and London: The University of Chicago Press, 1993

Colombo, John Robert. *The Dictionary of Canadian Quotes.* Toronto: Stoddart Publishing Company Ltd, 1991

Crook, Marion, and Nancy Wise. *How to Self Publish and make money: Writing, publishing and selling your book in Canada.* Kelowna, BC: Sandhill Publishing/Crook Publishing, 1997

Desauer, J.P. *Book publishing: A basic introduction.* New York: Continuum, 1989

Deval, Jacqueline. *Publicize Your Book!: An Insider's Guide to Getting Your Book the Attention It Deserves.* New York: The Berkley

Publishing Group, 2003

Garner, Joe. *Never forget the good times: A story of life in British Columbia*. Nanaimo, BC: Cinnibar Press, 1995

Holt, Robert Lawrence. *How to Publish, Promote & Sell Your Own Book*. New York: St. Martin's Press, 1985

Kremer, John. *1001 Ways to Market Books: for authors and publishers*. 6th ed. Fairfield, IA: Open Horizons, 2006

Levinson, Jay Conrad, Rick Frishman and Michael Larsen. *Guerrilla Marketing for Writers:100 Weapons for Selling Your Work*. Writer's Digest Books, 2001

Media Weavers. *Writer's Northwest Handbook*. 4th ed.

Nicholas, Ted. *How to Self-Publish Your Own Book & Sell a Million Copies*. Enterprise-Dearborn, 1993

Poynter, Dan. *The Self-Publishing Manual: How to write, print and sell your own book*. 10th ed. Santa Barbara, CA: Para Publishing, 1997

------. *Writing Nonfiction: Turning Thoughts into Books*. Santa Barbara, CA: Para Publishing, 2000

------. *Self-Publishing Manual Vol 2*. Santa Barbara, CA: Para Publishing, 2009

Poynter, Dan, and Mindy Bingham. *Is There a Book Inside You?: How to Successfully Author a Book Alone or Through Collaboration.*

Santa Barbara, CA: Para Publishing, 1985

Reiss, Fern. *The Publishing Game: Publish a Book in 30 Days!*. Boston: Peanut Butter and Jelly Press, 2003

------. *The Publishing Game: Bestseller in 30 Days!*. Boston: Peanut Butter and Jelly Press, 2003

Rogers, Geoffry. *Editing for Print.* Writer's Digest Books, Cincinnati: 1985

Ross, Tom, and Marilyn Ross. *Marketing Your Books: A collection of profit making ideas for authors and publishers.* Buena Vista, CO: Communication Creativity, 1990

------. *The Complete Guide to Self-Publishing.* 3rd ed. Cincinnati: Writer's Digest Books, Cincinnati: 1994

INDEX

A

Acknowledgement 59, 60
Advertising 51, 89, 137, 146, 148-150, 153, 155, 156, 162
Afterword 66
Author 2, 3, 6, 24, 34, 41, 47-49, 54, 59-61, 85, 88, 137, 166, 167, 168
Author photo 143

B

Back cover 43, 45, 51
Back matter 67
Bar code 45, 86, 87
BC Bookworld magazine 148
Binding 89, 113, 114
Blog 31, 161, 163
Book clubs 171
Bookkeeping 124, 126, 127, 130
Bookland EAN bar code 85, 86
Booksellers 6, 144, 149, 169, 170, 180, 182-184
Bookstores 6, 7, 16, 28, 40, 43, 45, 64, 66, 71, 72, 86, 89, 90, 118, 120, 132, 135, 138, 148, 153, 164-168, 175
BowkerLink 83
Business 5, 16, 19, 33, 38, 42, 53, 58, 80, 87, 90, 92, 95, 103, 109, 117, 119, 121, 123, 126, 129-132, 148, 153, 155, 158, 162, 168,

169, 170, 173, 176, 177, 179, 181, 187, 196-198

C

Canada Post 178
Canadian Copyright Office 77
Canadian Internet Registry Authority (CIRA) 158
Canadian Writer's Market 7, 28, 135
Cataloging in Publication (CIP) 80, 82
Consignment 181-183
Copyright 4, 9, 33, 49, 50, 52, 53, 76, 77, 95
Corporate sales 172
Cover 5, 8, 16, 41-43, 52, 89
Credit card 1, 128, 129, 180

D

Design 1, 8, 9, 11, 16, 41, 42, 53, 62, 66, 67, 72, 89, 143, 158, 167, 183
Desktop publishing 10, 11, 14, 55, 69, 94, 95, 99
Discounts 7, 164, 169, 170
Digital printing 108-110
Distributor 15, 83, 87, 120, 132, 140, 153, 164, 170-172
Domain 157, 158

E

Editing 4, 11, 35, 37-39, 89, 92, 167

Editor 1, 6, 9, 16, 39, 91, 190
Editors' Association of Canada 35
E-books 12, 13, 63, 110, 111, 157

F

Foreign rights 187, 171
Foreword 57-59, 82
Format 17, 41, 91, 94, 95, 157
Frontispiece 48, 54
Front matter 46

G

Galley 14, 91, 114, 136, 138
Glossary 55, 67, 68
GST/HST 121-124

H

History 10, 12, 27, 28, 40, 49, 51, 125
Hook 43, 44, 137, 145, 188

I

Index 14, 55, 67, 69, 95
Information sheets 139, 168
Introduction 59, 60, 81
Invoice 129, 176, 179
ISBN 9, 13, 45, 52, 78-81, 85, 140, 176

L

Laminate 114, 115
Legal Deposit 84
Libraries 41, 43, 45, 49, 64, 66, 69, 72, 81, 86, 95, 118, 119, 132, 135, 137, 149, 167-169, 175

M

Magazines 26, 40, 96, 136, 137, 143, 153, 155, 177, 187-189
Mailing lists 154
Mail order 71, 153, 154, 156, 175
Margins 96
Marketing 5, 6, 9, 89, 133, 134, 148, 151, 156, 159, 170, 171, 183, 184
Marketing plan 152, 163
Media 133, 134, 142, 146
Media packages 133, 136, 137, 142, 144
Memoir 21, 22, 25, 29, 30, 32, 40, 44

N

National Book Deposit 8
National Library of Canada 79, 81, 84, 85
New Book Service 82, 135
Newspapers 135-138, 145, 153, 155, 188
News release 134, 143, 145, 146, 161
Nom de plume 34

O

Order form 71, 72
Offset printing 104-107

P

Pen name 34
Poetry 38, 44
Preface 59, 60, 81
Press kit 142
Press release 142, 143, 146
Price 15, 88-90, 102, 140
Printers 51, 75, 89, 91, 101-107, 108, 115
Print-On-Demand (POD) 8, 9, 80, 104, 108, 109
Proof 112
Publicity 6, 132, 138, 146, 148, 155, 156, 166, 173, 183, 186, 195
Publisher 2-6, 12, 16, 21-24, 27, 31, 35, 36, 45, 48-50, 52, 53, 57,58, 68, 72, 79, 83, 84, 87, 88, 91, 92, 106, 109, 132, 139, 152, 163, 169, 170, 181, 187, 196
Purchase order 175

Q

Quill & Quire magazine 35, 149

R

Radio 142, 149, 187

Refund 7
Remainders 197, 198
Request For Quotation (RFQ) 107
Returns 164, 165
Reviews 42, 82, 83, 132, 135, 136, 138, 139, 144
Rights 186
Royalty 3, 4

S

Self-publish 3-5, 11, 13, 15-19, 21, 23, 26, 28-30, 32, 35, 39-41 51-53, 55, 71, 75, 79, 80, 87, 92, 102, 104, 105, 107, 109, 110, 112, 114, 115, 117-120, 125, 129, 130, 132, 136, 142, 150, 151, 155, 156, 161, 179, 171, 174, 180, 182, 185, 189, 191, 195
Seminars 191
Signings 166
Social networking 161, 163
Spin offs 193
Subsidy publisher 8-11, 27, 80
Subtitle 47

T

Table of contents 14, 55, 64
Tax 6, 84, 120, 127, 153, 177
Testimonials 23, 133
The Writers' Union of Canada (TWUC) 35
Title 5, 14, 15, 33, 56, 63, 65, 7998, 140
Title page 47, 53, 97

Typeface 62, 97
Typesetting 8, 11, 89, 93-96, 101, 123

U

UPC bar code 86

V

Vanity publisher 8

W

Website 15, 31, 63, 77, 109, 110, 121, 128,
134, 142, 153, 156-159, 161, 165, 177, 179,
195
Wholesaler 81, 169-171, 175, 180
Word of mouth 152
Workshops 191-193
Writer's Digest magazine 35, 48, 195
Writer's Market 138

Did you borrow this book?

Order a copy from your local bookstore or
order online at **www.selfpublishing.ca**

*"My husband and I borrowed your book from
the library and were so impressed we decided
to self-publish. We bought your book because
we need to consult it every day to go through
the process. We couldn't have done it without
your Self Publishing in Canada."*
Donna D'Amour
Publisher of *The Runaway and other stories*

FREE REPORT at www.selfpublishing.ca

Follow us on Facebook!
www.facebook.com/selfpublishingincanada